How to Eliminate Stress.

How to Eliminate Stress.

By

Marcel Limbasan

Library of Congress Cataloging in Publication Data.

ISBN 1- 58500-934-2

1stBooks rev. 5/31/00

About the Book

New breakthrough in stress research. New theory of stress. The new book : **"How to Eliminate Stress"** takes you into an unbeliavable journey from slavery to freedom, by showing you what stress really is, where it comes from, and how easily you could eliminate it from your life.

PREFACE.

"Necessity is the mother of invention"

This expression is universally accepted as truth, and like many others, I also had the chance to experience it to be true.

Born in Eastern Europe, from my childhood I have had to deal with many challenges from which I had many important lessons to learn. Though I came from a modest family, with limited financial possibilities, I always remember myself as a person interested in acquiring knowledge and wisdom. For some reason, I had this inner thirst to know more and more, and to appreciate the value of knowledge.

In 1984, I left Europe, and came to America, with the same hope that was burning in the hearts of millions of eastern Europeans, to find a better life. Leaving one kind of problems, and challenges behind, I had to face different ones here. And, because they were new for me, I also had to learn how to deal with them. The most painful challenge to deal with was "stress" I had no idea that the notion of stress is used in the medical domain. I knew about "stress" since I was in school, but only as a technical word, I was not aware of the fact that here in America, stress is seen as the root of most medical problems that people have to deal with. Being used to facing challenges and overcoming them, I became preoccupied with this subject, knowing that the most suitable person to deal with my high level of stress was myself. I was familiar with an old saying: "Give a command, and then do it yourself, if you want it to be done properly." So, I started to gather information in this area from most prestigious and well known specialists in this field, knowing that the best way to accomplish something fast, is to learn from the professionals. This is what I have done. Soon I realized that I am facing a new challenge: the top professionals in stress believe there is no cure for stress, an idea that I just could not accept. I always knew that, for everything I do, I am responsible. Stress is the result of a certain kind of behavior, and behaviors could be changed. I honestly could not accept the theory of stress as being realistic. So, I challenged myself to find the answer to this problem. I recalled the saying of Doug

Larson: "Some of the world's greatest feats were accomplished by people not smart enough to know they were impossible"

And after countless hours of personal studies, little by little I started to realize that stress is not an invincible enemy that was to control and affect people's life forever in a negative way.

And, pretty soon I started to understand what stress really is, how it works, and also how it could be eliminated. Once I understood that, I tested on myself, to see if it was going to work. And it did very well. Realizing the importance of a discovery like this, I felt its my duty to write this book and make it known to everybody who might be interested in a permanent solution for stress.

The major problem in dealing with stress today, is that since the present theory has been accepted as truth more than sixty years ago, most, if not all the professionals in this field, are not looking to challenge it, but to find a way to manage it, or get the best out of it. And of course that, if they believe that there is no cure for stress, they won't look for a solution for eliminating it.

But, if somebody will start to challenge this theory, he might be surprised to find out that it will not stand anymore to the latest tests. By reading the information contained in this book, you have the chance to prove to yourself that whatever I am writing is true, and by understanding and applying this simple information, the life that you improve is yours, and that of those whom you do love.

TABLE OF CONTENTS.

INTRODUCTION. 1

CHAPTER 1.   "REASONING" 13

CHAPTER 2.   LEARN HOW TO STOP PRODUCING STRESS..............29

WHO REALLY ARE THE STRESS ORS?...30
IS THE PAST REALLY GONE? 33
NEW VOCABULARY..35
POSITIVE ANCHORING. 37
SCREENING...42

CHAPTER 3.   "IMAGINATION". 45

THINGS THAT ARE UNCHANGABLE OR NON-SOLVABLE. 46
THINGS FROM THE PAST. 52
UNREALISTIC EXPECTATIONS OR UNFULFILLED DREAMS. 54
INNER NEEDS AND FEARS...57

CHAPTER 4.   A. THE "PROPULSION MECHANISM" 61

CHAPTER 5.   B. THE "SELF-DEFENSE MECHANISM"....................69

1.   THE SUBCONSCIOUS LEVEL 70
2.   THE CONSCIOUS LEVEL 73

CHAPTER 6.   "EMOTION". 79

CHAPTER 7.   HOW TO REMOVE THE STRESS 89

1.   REMOVING ONE AT A TIME, AS WE INDENTIFY IT. 92
2.   MAKING A LIST, AND TAKING ONE BY ONE. 94

CHAPTER 8.   MAKE UP YOUR MIND...103

Introduction.

Yes, the news of the century: "How to eliminate stress".

Could this be really true? Even though it might seem to be just a dream, after you have finished reading this information, you could see for yourself, that this "Plague of the century" has no more power over you, and you could do something about it. To do that is not going to cost you an arm and a leg. Just the desire to learn and apply simple principle's that you might already know, but were not aware of their importance. You all along had this possibility, and now the time has come to all of us to find it out.

Remember when you learned to speak, to write, to ride a bike, or to drive a car? Even though you may have learned these things long ago, you still are able to do them any time you want, don't you? Yes. The same thing happens with eliminating stress. Once you have learned how, you will never forget it. Eliminating stress is a learned habit, you could do it any time you feel you need it. It's as simple as that.

Now, for us to be able to eliminate stress, we first might need to get a basic understanding of three important things: What our body is, how it works, and important laws and principles that govern its function.

Knowing these things, we will be able to function the right way, and of course our journey in life will be a joyful one. The whole problem of stress lies in the fact that we sometimes inadvertently break some of these principle's, and as result, we get stressed. Let's take a simple example:

Suppose you just bought a brand new car. You took it home,

and you are very proud of it. Also, you have two children, one eighteen who already has a driver's license, and another who is only twelve.

What do you think is going to happen to the car if the older one takes it for a drive? Well, probably nothing bad. Having a driver's license, he knows basic things about the car, and how to use it properly. But, do you think that you have the same outcome if the younger one will get his hands on it? I don't think so. Why? Because he is a bad person, who wants to wreck the car? No, but because he does not know how to use it, he might wreck it without bad intention, and the damage is done, no matter if it is intentional or not. The same thing happens with our body. Despite our intentions, when we break the rules of our body function we experience discomfort, anxiety and stress. But, if we learn these rules and regulations, then we can apply them correctly, and as result we will experience peace of mind, and will be able to live a happy life.

There is a proverb that says: "We are what we eat" And basically this is true. The food that we eat daily is taken by our body and used to feed and regenerate itself. The kind of food we choose to eat determines the health of our body. If we are careful, and know what is good for us, we will be selective, and eat the foods that help us to develop a healthy body. If we do not care, and we start to over eat, or we have an imbalance eating habit, this will have a negative effect on our body, which will result in other side effects that will make our life less pleasant. Now, if the quality of our body depends upon the quality of the food we eat, it makes sense to believe, that the quality of our mind, also depends upon the quality of information that we are feeding it every day. We might not be aware of it, but as long as we are awake and alive, we are feeding our minds with all the information from the environment we are daily exposed to.

 The quality of this information will determine the quality of our thinking ability.

Realizing this principle, how many of us were exposed to information from which we could have learned how our mind works, and how properly to deal with stress? Most of us have no clue about this subject. Then, how in the world might we be able to know how to deal properly with stress?

Remember the example with the car and the kids? The twelve years old, has no idea how the car works, and the laws and principles that govern its operation. And of course, if he is the one to drive it, you better have a good insurance policy, because he is heading for a disaster.

So, we are not far from this kid who is going to wreck the car, not because he is a bad kid, but because he is missing the knowledge required to use it properly.

From this example, we can see the necessity to learn something different, to enlarge our knowledge about ourselves, and doing so, we will be in the position of being capable to eliminate stress. It does not require expensive medication, or a lot of money to invest, only a desire to learn how to master our own body, and use it for our benefit.

Well, if we think a little bit about our life, we can say that our whole purpose in life, is to learn to communicate with the environment in such a way that we become one with it, and our interaction with it becomes a source of happiness and joy. By environment, we could understand everything that surrounds us, and we have to interact with; which could be people, places or situations that we might come in contact with during our life. To do that, we were designed with a few abilities that might help us. When these abilities are used properly, our life becomes enjoyable. But, by the same token, when consciously or not, we are misusing any of these the results of course are unpleasant.

One of these unpleasant results is stress.

Basically, the environment is the same for all of us. The only thing is, that we humans, even though we have these abilities to communicate with the environment; because of our personal upbringing, the way we perceive the environment is affected by our culture, religion and other social factors.

So, many times, we get a distorted idea about how to deal with certain things, situations or people. And as result, we start to experience unpleasant situations or events that we might not know how to deal with.

That's why it's important to learn how to distinguish between reality and fiction, ideologies that make sense - and any time might be proved as such- and others that even though might be popular, do not have a real scientific, or logical basis.

 We live in a time when we are able to send a space ship millions and billions of miles away in space to search the wonders of our universe. And we also know that all these happenings are based on laws and principles that govern the functioning of our planet and universe. Not only that, but even our body, an unbelievable live mechanism, works based on certain laws and principles. The more we are aware of these, and respect them, the easier we might make our life, by avoiding things that might cause us harm.

Basically, the purpose of this information is, to help us understand that the relationship between ourselves and the environment we are dealing with every day, is based on specific laws and regulations that we need to know and obey, in order for us to be able to have a positive communication with it. We need to understand that we are a part of a unit. We just cannot survive independent of our environment.

To illustrate this let's look at a car. If you open the hood of the car you might see many components that help the car to function properly. Do you think that by pulling out one or more of these parts, let's say the carburetor, and putting it on the bench, will it help the car work better? Or worse? Of course it will not work better. It won't even start anymore.

Why is that? Because for the car to work properly, all the components must be in the right place, and function according to the designer's specifications. The car works as a unit, even though it is made up of many parts connected together. The same thing happens with us, as humans living on earth today. Aware or not, we are part of this unit we call earth. The only difference between us and the other components is the fact that we are a conscious part of it.

All the other components, alive or not, have a built in program to follow the necessary steps, so the earth works as a unit. Only we, who were designed to enjoy our life here, were equipped with something much superior than any others, the capacity of understanding the environment, and of choosing to do what we need to. So, let's start with what our body is.

We could safely say that our body is a very complicated live organism, which has many components, each of them playing a 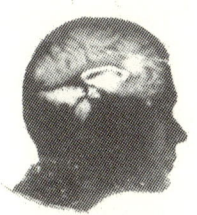 specific role in the proper functioning of the body as a whole. And like any other complicated organism, its functionality is based upon specific laws and regulations that we need to know, if we want to use our body the right way, or according to its specifications.

We already know that we have a brain, which is the main organ that controls all the body. And the brain also works based on specific laws and regulations. The better we know these, the easier it is for us to master the whole body. The brain is like a central computer that receives all the information from the environment. It arranges the information in files, and also based on the information, directs the body to act in a specific way.

Let's see now, how the brain receives information. Imagine a video camera. Most of us might own one. What does the camera basically do?

See, those people who invented the camera, have discovered, that there are certain materials around us that have some interesting properties. They could absorb and store information and maintain it in the original form, for a long period of time.

So, what the video camera basically does, is that it has the property of associating an audio information with a video information, and maintain this association in its original form on the tape or a disc, for a long period of time. And any time we want, we can see again the same information we have taped long ago. Now, the camera by itself will never change any information instead will preserve it unchanged, so we can review it at any time we might want to. Because the camera is an intelligence that is not alive, it will never give any meaning to this information. It is up to the person who sees them, to give them or not, a specific meaning. Basically, the same way our brains absorbs information. Through our senses, audio and video information that take place around us, are associated by our brain in what are known as neuron associations. Now, because we differ a bit from lifeless cameras, and being conscious of ourselves, we have the capacity to give a meaning to each of these associations. So, unconsciously we attach a meaning to these associations, and based on our own interpretation of this information, we store them as pleasure or pain producing files. All of them get stored in our memory, waiting to be retrieved and reviewed in the future. In other words, to any information from around us, we unconsciously attach a positive feeling or a negative one, based on our interpretation of it. Basically this is the way our brain absorbs information. And like the camera, the brain by itself will not modify any of this information, but, it will always retrieve it, the way it was originally stored.

Now let's see how does the brain processes the information which already was stored in the memory banks.

To illustrate this let's imagine a computer.

When we bought it, its memory was empty, except the pre installed programs and software installed in it. Once it is in our possession, it is up to us to put any information, which we might want in it. So, all the information that we put in it will be stored in files. Each file has its own name. Any time we want to retrieve any of the information or file, we turn on the computer, and access these files as many times as we want. Now, does the computer by itself, is going to change any of the information? Certainly not, it will keep this information unchanged, so we can access and review it, at our own will.

So, till now we saw, that our brain absorbs the information from our surroundings or the environment; we give a meaning to them, and then they are stored in our memory, as neuron associations between an audio video and a feeling. The feelings we attach to them, as we already mentioned could be positive or negative. The positivity or negativity is established by our own perception of the information, and not necessarily reflects the reality of the information.

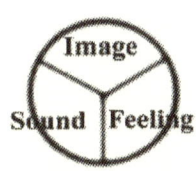

We know, that coming from different backgrounds, we have different opinions about many things. Some of us might consider some things being acceptable, some of us might not. So, I would like to repeat this:

The meaning we give to the information is based on our own interpretation of it, and not necessarily reflects the reality.

Let's take a simple example to illustrate this:

Suppose that you are a lady sitting on a bench in the bus stop, waiting for the bus, so you could go home. It's getting late, and is almost dark outside. Suddenly, you see a car pulling over, the right door opens, and you hear the driver's voice telling you to get in. There is nobody else around, and the voice does not sound friendly at all. What is going to be your reaction? Most probably you get scared, and start looking for a way out of this presumably negative situation. Once you get scared, many negative feelings start to go through your mind. But, are you sure that you are really in danger? Or, you just presumed it.

Well, the negative feeling you are experiencing, is not based on the reality, but on your own interpretation of it. It could possibly be, that your next door neighbor, passing by, on the way to his house saw you in the bus stop, and to do you a favor, wanted to give you a ride home. And, because yesterday he got a cold, his voice sounded a little bit strange. And in fact, the reality was totally different, than your own interpretation of it. Now, if you realize that he is not a stranger, as you previously thought, that negative feeling would go away pretty fast.

But, let's say that, you do not recognize him, and try to escape by running away. What kind of feelings would you have all this time? Of course negative ones. And even after you get home, in your mind you still believe that somebody in the bus stop has tried to kidnap you.

So, remember: The way you feel is based on the meaning you give to the information which not necessarily might reflect the reality. This is a very important principle to keep in mind, because unknown to us, this is the root of many stressful situations.

See, as long as we live, constantly our mind receives information from the environment, and gives a meaning to it. And then, it "goes in our memory to be stored there."

So, the more negative meaning we give to the information from around us, the more negative associations "we store in our memory."

Up till now, we saw that our mind absorbs the information from around us like a video camera. Then, once the information get into our mind, the brain processes it like a computer does dividing it in files. And of course, in the same time, we continuously give a meaning to each of these bits of information, by "attaching a feeling" to them, which could be negative or positive, depending on our own opinion about them. This is a very important to learn, because by understanding this, it will be much easier to realize what stress is, and how we could avoid to produce more, and also how to eliminate it.

The general idea about stress is that going through our life, we encounter situations that are stress producers. And many professionals in this area teach people how to manage these situations in such a way, that they might reduce the stressful effect of the situation might have over them. So, what they basically say is that the situations are stress ors. Well, if that is the case, then how come many people go through repeat cycles of stress even though they might be home doing nothing, or they are not going through difficult situations, and yet still feel stressed? Contrary to the old idea the stress is nothing else, but our own product, as result of the negative meaning we might give to any particular situation. The truth of the matter is, that the state of stress, has at its roots two sources:

New stress, which is made by the person on the spot, and old stress, that was made in the past and "stored in our memory", and comes into the present when we are reviewing some files from our memory. Knowing this, in order to eliminate stress forever, we need to learn two things:

A. Learn how to stop producing new stress.
B. Learn how to eliminate the stress that already "have been stored in our memory".

Once we master these two things, it is guaranteed we will become a stress free person.

Before we start to do this, let's first see some of the characteristics or laws that governs the functionality of our brain. By learning these first, we will be able to understand better how the stress could be easily eliminated.

Now, let's talk a little bit of the third thing we should know. There are a few important characteristics, actually three, which we need to learn how to use properly, if we want to become stress free persons.

Of course, our brain has many more characteristics, but we will discuss the ones that are related to our subject. For this, imagine a three links piece of chain. They might be three pieces, but they form a single unit.

Imagination

Reasoning   **Emotion**

1. One is **REASONING.**

2. Second is **IMAGINATION.**

3. Third is **EMOTION.**

By "Reasoning" ability, we might understand the capacity of understanding the environment or any other information that we might come in contact with, accepting or rejecting any of it, and passing a judgment on it as being positive or negative.

This ability is specific to humans only. None of the other creatures on earth posses this ability. Being able to reason our own environment, we can choose to differentiate between things, accepting or rejecting them based on our free will. In other words, unlike the animals that have a built in program how to instinctively react to the environment, we have this ability to exercise our free will in deciding how to react to the outside stimuli. Used properly, this ability helps us to develop as normal and successful human beings. Improperly used, it brings unpleasant consequences.

To illustrate the second characteristic, we will use a simple illustration: Imagine a calculator. Most of us are using it, or at list we have one at home someplace.

Why did you buy a calculator? Well, most probably you trust that this small piece of plastic could do math much faster than you do. Don't you? You don't have to be shy. We all got one for the same reason. Now, how come that a simple piece of plastic that could not talk, or even walk, or do a smallest thing that we might do, is capable to do math much faster then we do?

Well, those guys who invented it found out that there are some materials that are capable to combine certain information, according to some specific laws that do not change, and give right answer to this information.

Isn't that something? Yes it is. And it does not matter how many times you use them always you get the right answer.

One of our brain characteristics is to do something like that, yet even more than that. A calculator needs somebody to turn it on, and to punch the numbers in, to be able to function, and unless a human being does that, the most powerful calculator is worth nothing. But our brain does not need a battery or somebody else to turn it on and off.

We as conscious human beings, have this capacity to combine not only numerical information, but any kinds of information, and ask our mind to process them. And guess what? Our mind is capable to give us the best answer. Of course, the quality of the response depends on the quality of the information that we have "stored in our mind" in that specific area.

This characteristic is what we commonly call "Imagination."

It is a property of our mind to combine any kind of information, and give us a result, based on the quality of the information that we previously fed our mind with in that specific area.

Remember the saying: " Garbage in, garbage out".

We feed our mind with quality information we get quality results, but if we do not care what kind of information enters our mind, do not be surprised that we come up with unsatisfactory or even bad results.

An improper use of this ability is the major source of stress for most of the people today.

The third, but not the least ability that we have, is the capacity to consciously feel the result of the information that we previously accepted and combined, no matter if they were negative or positive.

If we have chosen to accept positive information and combined these, as a result we most probably feel a positive emotion. On the other hand if we accepted and combined a negative information most probably we feel a negative emotion.

I say most probably because we have the choice of giving any meaning to any kind of information no matter what they really are.

The quality of the emotion depends not on the quality of the information, but on the meaning we might give to the information, which could be positive or negative. And based on the meaning we give, we will feel it as a positive or negative emotion.

This ability is commonly known as emotion .

Let's take a simple example to illustrate this. Let's imagine a simple radio. We know that the radio has an antenna through which absorbs from the air radio waves, and then transforms these waves into sounds by the use of a speaker that is built into the radio.

So the vibration of the speaker with the sound produced by it  is the " emotion." The same way our body absorbs from the environment information that is combined by our brain, and then we feel them through what we call emotions. Now the radio itself will not give any interpretation of the waves received, but what they exactly are, but we as humans have the ability to interpret the information we absorb from the environment and give them the meaning we want. By doing this we can change the emotion we will feel. Because the quality of the emotions that we will feel is determined by the meaning we give the information, and not the quality of information. That's why there is a big truth in the proverb that says:

"Whatever you decide to believe it becomes true for you"

Understanding this fundamental truth will help us to really eliminate stress, because stress is a negative emotion that is the result of our giving a negative meaning to a specific information or part of environment. Knowing that we have the power to choose the meaning of any information, then it's up to us to learn how to do that, and once this becomes a habit, we will unconsciously do it any time it's necessary. Of course that the results will be positive, and the stress will be no more. So like the other two abilities, this one too, properly used, can be beneficiary to us. But by the same token, improper use of it might result in stressful situations.

Now, let's take one ability at the time, and see both sides of them. In other words, how using them properly will result in a happy life, and also, the side effects, and the damage that might result from an improper use of them.

   **Or**

Chapter 1.

Let's start with the first one:

1. "REASONING"

Superior to any other creature on the earth today, we humans were equipped with this ability to understand our own environment, and give a meaning to it. And by having this faculty, we are able to enjoy and live a happy life. We can look around us, and see the beautiful earth, full of wonders that please our senses. We take these things for granted, not realizing how lucky we are, to be able to manifest this ability. Take for example, the most beautiful picture, and show it to a dog, or cat, or to a horse to see what they think about. You may be amazed at its beauty, but they have no reaction of appreciation or any other, except maybe to use it to play, or even eat it.

See, the variety of colors, the shapes and forms that our environment is made of, makes it possible for us to enjoy it through this ability of reasoning. To look at the environment, to feel it, to smell, or taste it, and by doing that we are able to live a joyful life.

Sounds like a paradise, but then why still do we have so many problems in the world today, and talking about our subject, why is that millions of people today, are experiencing more and more stress in their life?

Now, this ability of reasoning is of great benefit to us, if we use it properly. Unaware, many times we might misuse it, and of course then the results will be different.

Let's take a simple example to illustrate this:

We all know about cars. They were designed by the manufacturers to be used by people, and by doing so, to simplify and make their life better. But, did you know that today, cars are one of the major causes of death? Now, can we say that the cars are bad? Or, that the manufacturers of the cars had bad intentions in their mind, when they designed them? And, can they be blamed for the death of those people killed in car accidents? Everybody will agree that's not the case. The reality is, that the misuse, or improper use of them, are the cause of the accidents. More than that, we all know that all cars are equipped with some safety devices, or systems that might prevent an accident, such as the brake system, or the signal system, horn and so on. All these, for the sole purpose of avoiding danger, and making the usage of it, safer and enjoyable. So, the same thing happens with this ability of reasoning. We can use it properly, and as a result, we enjoy a beautiful life. Or, we can, for some reason misuse it, and of course then the result is different. And, one of the undesired results is stress. Before we go into how the misuse of this ability might result in stress, let's answer another question about it. Why were we, out of all the others creatures on the earth today, we alone were equipped with this kind of ability? There are many theories about human existence. Some have its roots in religion, some in science. A simple way, that will help us to understand the reality of human existence, is by using common sense. Let's see, how can we do that. Suppose, that during your vacation you visited many beautiful places, and among them a place with a huge aquarium. There, you saw many kinds of fish, big and small, beautiful and ugly, in other words a variety of marine creatures.

Impressed by their beauty, you start desiring to have an aquarium of your own, so you could be able to enjoy them, any time you want. After you get home, you start planning how to do that, right? First, you look for the right place in the house. You want them to have enough light, the right temperature, in other words, the right environment where to place the aquarium.

Once you did that, you go to the store and start buying all the necessary things that are needed. The aquarium, water plants, rocks, water filter, thermometer, a light, fish food, and all the other accessories are needed. Then, after all are ready and in their right place, you go ahead, and get the fish and put them in. Once everything is done, you could rest, and enjoy your work.

14

Now, if some of your friends come to your house, after you did all this job, and look at your beautiful project, what do you think should would be their reaction?

Most probably will be amazed to see such a variety of fish living in a friendly environment, and enjoying their life in it. Even though none of them were present when you did this project, what do you think will be the right answer to the question: How did all of these come about?

Some of them could believe one thing; the others, another, but by simply using common sense, by looking at this project, can they safely say that everything appeared out of nothing, and kept evolving, till became what it is? Or, they can say that, because of the way everything is arranged and functions, this is a wonderful project, which has a loving and kind designer.

Which of these two interpretations corresponds better to our situation? We don't have to be a rocket scientist to recognize the real one.

Now, let's go back to our subject and look around us, to our environment, to "the huge aquarium," the universe. By taking a closer look at it, we can easily see, that it just cannot be the product of an accident. All the laws that govern its functionality, are too perfect and work too well, to be something, that just happened to come about, out of nowhere.

Let me ask you a little question:

If you go into the jungle, where people are way behind in technology, and they live a primitive form of life; how fast these people drive their cars on the freeway, and if they get a speed ticket for that?

You must be crazy you may say. There are no freeways in the jungle, and these people don't know how to drive a car. And there are no highway patrol officers there to give them a ticket. It is ridiculous to believe that.

But, why is ridiculous to believe that?

Because the cars, and the freeways, are the product of a designer, they do not just grow, or evolve in the jungle. These people have to be taught, and trained how to build these things in the jungle, so there must be somebody to teach them, who already has the knowledge and experience.

You might come with the argument, that our whole society, long ago was in that primitive stage, and that it developed into what we see today. That is truth, but did these peoples created or designed, any of the laws and principles, they have used in their developing?

Or, they just discovered, and use them for their benefit. See, there is one thing, when somebody provides you with the environment, and the necessary tools and equipment, so you can use them to build something, and it is a totally different thing when you have nothing. No laws, no principles, no equipment and you start to build something without them. See, even the smartest rocket scientist, can't do something with nothing. It's easy for a cook to prepare a tasty meal when he could go to the market and buy all he needs for it, but what kind of food would that be, when there is no cook with the knowledge, or the right ingredients? Today, some of the scientists argue, that under the right environment, with the right ingredients, life could have been developed, out of, kind of nothing. But, let's ask them how much, and how complicated the environment, and how much the ingredients would have to be to put them in the right place, at the right time, maintain them for period of time, until that little form of life could develop a life of its own; and live long enough, till it might transform itself into another more sophisticated form of life, and eventually becomes what today is, the powerful and capable human brain. Who was the one to provide, build and maintain that environment, long enough so this process of evolution might take place?

Remember: In the beginning there was nothing, no laboratory, no scientists, NOTHING.

Tell them, honestly to answer these questions.

 Who would have this kind of capacity, billions of billions of years ago?

There were no special laboratories, with expensive equipment and specialists, to make sure that nothing might go wrong. Then, honestly, how could their theory possibly be true?

The reality is, that as we mention before, anything that we believe to be true, becomes true for us.

So, many of today's scientists, getting used to so much of the evolution theory; for them it became truth long ago, and what they are doing now, are looking for something, or anything that might sustain it. But if they were to be challenged, to really find the truth, might find themselves empty handed.

Another reason why many scientists are sustaining this theory of evolution is because of the bad name that religions give to the reality of human existence. And many of these scientists cannot believe the variety of religious interpretations, so the other alternative that remains, is evolution.

But, if the religion in general is responsible for this big mess, it does not mean that there is not an intelligent designer behind this beautiful universe.

And as a matter of fact, the true religion has to agree with the real science. The problem today comes from the fact that the science and religion are kind of two enemies that divide people, and set the stage for a rivalry between people who accept religion as their guide, and people who accept science as their guide. The truth is, that they should have the same common goal, to find the simplest way toward finding our common history, and also, our common future. They should unite their forces in finding the truth, because we all are humans, no matter what our beliefs are.

We all have the same desires and aspiration, toward a better and longer life. So, basically we are looking for the same thing. Why not let the religious truth, combined with the real science, help us all to see the reality of our existence. This is what we basically try to do here. Recognize and understand, that as wonderful human beings, we are the product of an intelligent and powerful Designer. And realizing that, we need to understand how we were designed to function, and by doing that, we surely live our life to the fullest.

See, the specialists in stress believe, that as long as we live, we are subject to stress, and unless we die, we cannot get rid of it. This implies that, we were designed with this so call "disease", by whoever designed us. If we were to come out of an evolution, how come this came about, and how come the primitive forms of life could survive, being exposed to the unfriendly environment, long enough to transform themselves into a different form of life?

If we just reason a little bit, it is impossible to be so. On the other hand, if we were the product of a intelligent designer, with the purpose of living forever, it makes sense to believe, that if somebody has the knowledge and power to set up the whole universe, with all its laws and regulations that are working perfectly for billions of years, He would be smart enough to realize, that stress is an enemy of his human creation, and exposing humans to daily stress will shorten their life span, and make it miserable, instead of getting positive results from it. If you were that powerful designer, would you do that? I don't thing so. The reality is, that stress is not a "disease", but something that we ourselves are producing by improper usage of some of our faculties. And once we learn to stop doing that, then stress disappears. It's as simple as that. And, the only way to be able to achieve this is by recognizing these faculties of ours, how they work, and by learning to use them properly.

Now, going back to our main subject "Reasoning", let's see how practically, we can use this faculty the right way. And by doing that, we eliminate "the old stress", and also we will stop creating new ones.

If we take a closer look around us, we can see that we have at least two sides in most things. We have good and bad, black and white, day and night, right and wrong, tall and short, big and small, negative and positive, pessimist and optimist, and so on. Now, we can recognize that these two are opposed to each other, and by being opposed they have opposite results or effects when they are used. So, every day we use our faculty, and reason which one of these is better for us. When we choose properly, the results are positive, but, by the same token, when we choose something improper, we cannot expect that the result to be still positive. It will be most probably negative, and in many cases will result in stress.

We know that basically, there are two kinds of people, some who are optimists, and some who are pessimists. Now, all are going through many kinds of situations in life. But the way they go through them, differs a lot. Why is that? Well, we have mentioned before that we are equipped with another faculty that is imagination, through which we are constantly combining any kind of information. And of course, the quality of information influences the quality of results.

If we are a pessimistic person, we have the tendency to combine negative information, and we get negative results, and many of them will result in stress. If we are an optimistic person, we have the tendency to combine positive information, and of course that the results will be positive.

So, here is the key: We need to learn this, believe as truth and once we do that, it will become true for us. Then an amazing thing is going to happen. We will start to recognize easily negative information, and its negative results, and we will be able to use the faculty of reasoning to reject this bad old habit of combining negative information. And little by little, our attitude will change, from a pessimistic, to an optimistic one. If anybody is to make a survey to see what kind of persons are more stressed, guess what? The reality is that all pessimists are people with a high degree of stress, and on the other hand, the stress level of the ones that are optimists is somewhere close to zero.

We mentioned earlier, that our mind continuously absorbs information from the environment, and based on our own interpretation, we attach a meaning to it. And, we do not have to be a rocket scientist, to recognize that people who are pessimists, though they may not be aware of it are continuously attaching negative feelings to the information they encounter from the environment. Once they did so, these neuron associations, are placed for "storage" in their memory. And of course, that when these are recalled, they start to feel that negative feeling. Unaware that this is a part of a negative memory, they blame the feeling on the environment. That's why almost everybody today, believes that we get stress because we are facing stress ors, which have a stressful effect over us.

On the other hand, the optimistic ones, looking at things through a positive attitude are attaching positive feelings to this information. The results are totally different.

Anytime when they recall this information, they are not producing any stress.

Let's take a simple example to illustrate this:

First, you are aware that you are a normal person, with a normal mind, aren't you? And, your answer will most probably be: Yes. Now, a normal person, with a normal mind, when asked a question, what should he normally do? Answer the question in a normal manner. This is something natural to be so. But let's say, that I ask you this question:

Please, tell my about a very positive experience you had when you were fourteen years old, and give me some details about it. And as a normal person, you start to tell me about this exciting experience you had in the past.

Now during your explanation, what kind of state of mind do you start to experience? Unaware, you start to feel good, and relive some of those wonderful feelings that were stored in your memory for so long; and now even though years later, you feel them again. Now, how come that I asked you a simple question and this changed your mood, making you to relive wonderful feelings from the past? As we mentioned before, when, a person is asked a question, he should answer the question in a normal manner. Why is it that you didn't answer it in a normal manner, but you started to answer in a positive state of mind and happiness?

The answer is not that you are abnormal, but my question triggered in your mind certain memories, that have attached to them some positive feelings. You start to see in your mind, the people and places you were many years ago, and of course, beside these video and audio information, that you are reliving, you start to feel also the positive feelings, that you had attached to them long ago.

Now let me ask you another question:

Please tell me about a negative experience you had when you were seventeen?

Well, once you start telling me about this negative experience, I could see from here that your previous smile starts to disappear from your face, the tone of voice changes, and by the time you finished your experience, I could see that your mood is more negative, rather than normal or positive. Why is that? Is your mind normal? Yes. But, then why not just answer the question without the negative feelings? See, you are still a normal person, but my question triggered this time totally different kind of memories. So, these memories having attached to them some negative feeling in the past, unaware of, you start to feel them again, and they are the ones that changed your mood, not the present or the environment, like most of us might think. And this is basically a major source of stress. To unconsciously retrieve and relive many of our past memories, to which we have attached in the past a negative feeling. Because this process happens instantly, we blame it on the environment, as the source of stress.

And of course that does not matter how hard we work on this, we will never be able to eliminate stress. For the simple fact that we are working in the wrong direction. What we should be doing is, to accept how our mind processes information, and to work in removing these negative feelings that we have attached in the past to many of our memories. And by doing

21

that, anytime when we might recall any of the past experiences without a negative feeling attached to them, there is no more stress, but a memory with no negative effect over us. It is as simple as that.

As we mentioned before, people who are pessimists or negativists, are attaching more often negative feelings to the experiences they go through, unaware of the fact that this information will be "saved in their memory banks", and will be retrieved later. Of course later on, when retrieved, they have a stressful effect over them.

On the other hand, the optimists ones or the positivists are attaching a positive feeling to their experiences, and of course, they are storing positive feeling with these memories, which later on, when retrieved and relived, will create a positive mood for them.

Now, how exactly can we change our attitude, from a negative to a positive?

The first step is **"AWARENESS"**

The second step is **"DESIRE"**

The third step is **"DECISION"**

The fourth step is **"MOTIVATION"**

The fifth step is **"DISCIPLINE"**

Overlooked by many people today, awareness plays an important factor in the habit changing process. Some people might desire to change, but first they need to be aware of the fact that they have a choice, and they could do something about it. Most of today's poor people are living like that because nobody made them aware that they could really change their status.

See, the secret is, that unless somebody is aware of something, he will never develop a desire to change, or to obtain that something.

But, once somebody is aware of having a choice, that they could make, many of them, start to desire to change. So, till now you were not aware of the fact that you might be able to eliminate all the stress that is making your life more or less miserable.

By reading this information, you realize that you have a choice now. And, you could take a decision to ignore it, or you could start to develop a desire to do something about it. And to help you a little bit, I want to give you a little hint. There is no other human on earth, more capable to solve your stress situation, than yourself. Remember that! So, it is your responsibility to do something about it. You know yourself better, and care more about yourself than anybody, so take the necessary steps to eliminate the stress that is making your life unpleasant, or even miserable.

Do not wait for a miracle pill, because your stress is your own creation. Sometime during your past, you "learned how to create it", now it is the time to learn how to eliminate it.

By "learn to create it" I mean that you, like any other person on this earth, unaware of, learned some bad habits, and by practicing them, they resulted in stress.

So, by "eliminate it", I mean, learn new habits of creating a positive feeling, instead of negative one, which is the root of stress.

See, in order for anybody to develop a desire, they must first increase the level of awareness to such a stage so that it becomes reality for them. In other words it should become truth for them.

How this could come about? We may say? Reality is created through validation. To validate something, we need to have enough credible information that we could trust, and once we do that, it becomes truth for us. Being accepted as truth, then we could develop a strong and durable desire to obtain that particular thing or information.

Let's take a simple example to illustrate that:

Let's say that you own two houses, which you have bought ten years ago.

At that time, because the economy was in a bad shape and it was the buyers market, you paid much less than they were worth.

23

Now, the economy being in better shape, the value of the houses increased considerably.

One day, after you came home from work, you found a message on your answering machine from one of your friends, who is a real estate broker. He wants to know if you will sell the house that you are renting, because he has somebody interested in it.

Now, you talk it over with your wife, and because the economy is still in pretty good shape, decide to still keep it for a while. So, you call him and tell him that. Hearing your answer he tells you:

I am your friend, and my job is to sell houses, but I would like you to know, that now is the best time to sell. Because about four months ago, the house prices started slowly to go down, and it looks like they will keep going down. So, before you start losing from the equity you have accumulated during these years, the best thing is to sell now. Think about it and get back to me later.

Now, there are no signs of recession, and to you the economy looks good; you don't feel like selling. Although the warning was pretty serious, you still are not going to believe it, but also you cannot afford to ignore it. So, the best thing you find to do is to look for more information in this subject.

And you start to check the records on the houses sold in the last few months. Once you see that they sold a little bit under their value, than you might believe it. If you still want more proofs, you might wait another month or two, and see if the prices keep going down, or they come back to normal. If the prices keep going down, it is time for you to believe it. Once you really believe it, the desire to sell will follow. So, you take the decision to sell.

See, as we mentioned before, the reality is created through validation. Once we have enough information that we could really trust, we start to believe it as truth. And believing it as truth, we will start to desire to do something about it. But, unless we have sufficient information that we could rely on, we will not develop a strong desire that could trigger a decision to change.

So, in our situation we need to look to find real information, which we can count on. And once we find it, we will be able to check the accuracy, so our decision is based on real facts, not just on somebody's opinion.

For more than half a century people all around the earth were taught, that as long as we live we cannot get rid of stress. And like good listeners, everybody accepted this ideology as truth. But my question to you is: How many of you who believe this ideology, really found enough proof for it, so you could validate it? Or you just accepted it, because it was taught in schools, or the therapist told you that?

Did you know that more than a billion people are taught that the communism is the best society, and their interest is to extend it to the rest of the world? But, how many of us in a free society believe that? Probably none.

So, the truth of the matter is, that we should validate our reality based on enough truthful information that we get, not necessarily to believe it because many others are doing the same. We might be right, but also we might be wrong.

And, when it comes to stress, we better look for an update in this subject, and look honestly for the truth, and then we can validate our reality, in such a way that we might benefit from it.

I think, that if it make sense to everybody, we better look for the truth in this matter, instead of holding on to the ideology that has been here for so long, and made us slaves of something that we could eliminate so easily. Till now there was no information on how to eliminate stress, and all of us were under understanding that there is no cure for it. But no more, the only thing you need to do is, try to find out if these information's are true or not.

Once you find out, then the desire for change will develop automatically. So, you have nothing to lose, but only to gain.

As we have seen from this information, the desire that results in a decision, has to be validated for ourselves as truth. The more information we are exposed to, the higher the level of awareness. The higher the level of awareness, the stronger the desire that will result in a decision.

So, basically we need to repeatedly absorb through repetition of the information, and then it becomes familiar to us, and of course acceptable, and eventually powerful enough to act upon, by taking the next necessary steps to accomplish our purpose.

Remember when you were in school? You were given homework, to learn about a certain subject, right? What you were taught to do? Go home, study the material more than once, and by repeating it many times it becomes familiar to you, so you could be able to answer the right way, when you might be asked later on.

But, unless you became familiar with the subject, you had a hard time to recall and apply the information required. So, the better prepared you were from home, the easier for you at school, and the better the grades. Even though we are talking about a serious problem like stress, to eliminate it, we need to go through the same process of learning, like we used throughout our life, when we had to learn anything of value. Repeat it to ourselves, till it becomes familiar to us, and then use it as a formed habit, anytime we might need it.

As we mentioned before, for this to become powerful enough to push us to take the next steps to accomplish it, it must be validated as truth for us. And for that we need to have convinced ourselves with enough information that this is truth.

Remember, stress is your own creation, so it is your responsibility to learn a new habit to eliminate it. And once the habit is formed, it will be triggered by our mind, anytime necessary to eliminate, or avoid stress or things that might cause stress.

Let's take an example to illustrate this:

You remember the example with the two children. One is eighteen, and the other twelve. Now if the older one takes the car for a drive, and suddenly he sees that the brake lights from the car that is in front of him start flashing, what do you think he will do? For sure, if he pays attention to the road, he will step on the brakes too, because he knows that if the car in front of him stops he has to do the same, or he risks to get involved in an accident. And he does this anytime it is necessary, because when he learned to drive the car, he developed a habit to respond to any situation in the right manner, so he could be able to use the car properly.

Now, what do you think will happen, when the youngest one take the car for a drive?

Well, unless he is born a professional driver, and has the driving abilities in his genes, not having these habits of reacting properly, his mind will not trigger any adequate reaction when he sees the brake lights flashing.

And of course, that most probably is going to wreck the car. But, once he learns later on in life, he could develop a habit of reacting properly, and then it comes as something normal to react that way.

The same thing happens, when it comes to eliminating stress. Once we learn this habit, it becomes normal for us to react the right way. We will do it with ease.

So, let's remember what we have learned till now:

First, we get stressed not because of the environment, whatever it might be, or the so call stress ors.

Second, our mind continuously associates audio, video information, to which we attach a feeling, which could be negative or positive, based on our personal choice.

Third, all these neuron associations are stored in our memory banks, for later retrieval.

Fourth, to understand and give a meaning to the information coming from the environment, our mind uses a feed back process, in other words goes back in our memory banks to find a match for the new information. Once a match is found we instantly give a meaning to the new information.

Fifth, to many pieces of past information, we previously have attached a negative feeling, and when these kinds of " files" are retrieved, we start to remember the video and audio information that we have stored in that particular neuron association, but also we start to feel the feeling that was attached to it in the past.

Sixth, because we many times give negative meaning to the same kind of information after a while these retrieved files

27

contain so much negative feeling attached to them, that when retrieved later, they have a strong negative effect over us.

Seventh, because all this process happens instantly, and we are not physically transported back in time, we get the impression that the environment, or information caused us to feel this negative feeling, which we call stress.

Now that we are aware of these matters, let's see what is the solution. And it consists of two parts.

A. Learn how to stop producing stress.

B. Learn how to get rid of old stress, which is "stored in our memory".

Let's take one at the time:

Chapter 2.

Learn How to Stop Producing Stress

We can safely say, that there are about five steps we need to look at, and learn how to master, in order to be able to stop producing stress:

1. The first step is to recognize that the causes of stress are not, the so call "stress ors", but ourselves.
2. The second step, is to recognize the way our mind recalls information from our memory, and once recalled we start to "relive them", feeling the same kind of mental state we had previously attached to them.
3. The third step is to learn to avoid abusive or negative speech, knowing that they have attached to them a negative feeling, and when we use them, we also most probably feel these also.
4. The fourth step is to start looking at things and situations from a positive perspective, and doing this, we unconsciously attach to them a positive feeling, which in the future when retrieved will cause no stress, but a positive feeling.
5. The fifth step is to learn how to filter the information that we come in contact with, and even though it might be negative or bad for us, it will no longer trigger any negative feeling in us.

Now let's take one at the time and see how we can do that:

1.   The first step:

WHO REALLY ARE THE STRESS ORS?

Even though the general idea in the scientific community is that the so call "stress ors" are responsible for our getting stress; the truth of the matter is, that the stress that we encounter daily, is our own product, caused by us, and not by the environment.

See, there is a tendency of many of us, that once we believe something, to keep believing it. And taking it for granted it never crosses our mind to see, if that particular thing is truth, or not.

The same thing happens with the theory of stress.

Did you know that this theory is more than half a century old? And since then everybody accepted it without questioning it? Well, if somebody today, after so many years would want to honestly question it's validity, he might be surprised, as I was, to find out that there is something wrong with it. Maybe then it was easily accepted, because we didn't know so much about how our mind and body work. But today after so many new understandings of the wonders of our mind, there is no way that this theory will stand to an honest, and serious test.

The problem stands in the fact that all the professionals in this field grew up believing in it. They accepted it as truth without questioning it, so they were not prepared to challenge it.

And of course, that for them, there is no cure in sight.

But, if we start to understand the truth, then things start to change, and then we could eliminate stress.

Few years ago, one of my kids, his name is Nathan, had a habit of blaming others for something he did, and didn't want to be responsible for. So, one day when I asked him:

Nathan, do you have any idea who could have done this?

They made me do it, daddy, he answered me.

I looked at him, and smiled. Then calling him away from the others, I asked him:

Nathan, do you want me to believe, that such a smart and intelligent boy like you, let others make you do this? You are smart enough to know better, aren't you?

Yes, he tells me. Of course, I know better

Then, pretty soon after that, when the same kind of things happened, I asked again Nathan about it. Now the answer was totally different:

Daddy, I did it because of them.

Now, we might laugh at this, but it was the first step in the right direction. And more than that, he got the point from the first time. He realized that he did it, and improved. Of course, the behavior didn't change completely, on the spot, but the first step to recognize that everything he does, he does it, and is responsible for it.

We all know, that most of the kids, to get out of trouble, blame others, but did you know, that most of us grew up and even as adults, we still do the same? And as a proof, is stress. Any person that gets stressed does the same thing, which is to find who's to blame for it.

What do I mean by this?

Well, ask anybody: Why do you get stressed? Each of them will tell you:

Because of them. In other words the stress ors. Not me, the stress ors. And we start to blame everything around us, the weather, the job, the family, the bills, and so on. Is it their fault because I am stressed. Well, as we can clearly see now, that it's just not true anymore.

But you can still hold on to the old idea, or you could realize that: YOU are stressing yourself because of them.

This is the first step. Once you recognize that, there is a question that will come right away in your mind:

Should I still let them keep controlling the way I feel? Or should I do something about it? Remember the medical proverb:

"Proper diagnostic is half the cure".

So, after we are able to find the real cause, it is relatively easy to do the rest.

See, we cannot solve a non-solvable, but we surely could a solvable. And now knowing the real cause of stress, the problem becomes solvable. So, the next step is to see which is the better way to deal with it. We have switched the focus, from the stress ors over which we have little or no control, to the real cause, that we can control, ourselves. In other words, we start to become responsible for our state of mind.

2. The second step:

IS THE PAST REALLY GONE?

This is a very interesting question that we might ask ourselves, because knowing the truth about it will help us to eliminate stress.

We know, that the notion of time is understood in three stages: past, present and future.

The past we already went through, the present we are living it now, and the future is the one to come. As human beings, aware of our own existence, our mind records all the information that we receive from the environment, as long that we are awake and alive. And, even though we are not aware of it, these pieces of information are "stored in our memory banks" as neuron associations.

They all go into our subconscious mind, and form the database, that the brain uses when it needs to take a decision. The subconscious mind arranges this information in files, the same way that a computer does. And any time when some information is requested, the subconscious mind opens one of the files that contain that particular information. And of course we have to deal with whatever we have put in previously.

If we fill our mind with negative information, this is what is going to come out. On the other hand, if we are careful what kind of information enters our mind, of course that, when retrieved, these will be the same kind. This is what we commonly call memory. We all have it, and use it every day. And we all know, that we cannot remember a positive thing when we put in our memory a negative one, and by the same token, if we put in a positive thing, this is what we are going to remember.

So, basically we can say that the past is really gone, but our mind uses the information that we have from the past, in the decision making process, that we have to do in the present.

That's why we see many people today, who "are living in the past". They cannot differentiate between the events of the past that are gone, and never will come back, and the recorded events from our mind, which are used by the brain for reference. And they are working hard trying to change the past, and as result, there is a high degree of stress.

Also, beside the fact that many want to change the past, they are the ones that, by recalling negative memories from the past, get stressed reliving these negative feelings that they previously have attached to this information.

So, you take your pick: You could keep getting stressed, by reliving over and over, the same negative past memories, or you can realize that the past is gone, and let your mind use these only as reference, without any stressful effect over you. Most probably you will choose the second option, it sounds much better.

3.   The third step:

NEW VOCABULARY.

As we have mentioned before, we have the faculty of reasoning, which we are using daily, when we interact with the environment.   And we know we have a choice in the meaning we give to the information that comes from the environment.   Of course, based on the meaning we give to the information, we are creating a positive, or negative state of mind for ourselves.   And in our communication with others or the environment, we use words to define different things, situations and feelings.

So beside the choice of a meaning we give to the information, we also have a choice in the words used to define them.   For example, we can be persons with a very clear, rich, and positive vocabulary of words.   Or, we might not be too careful with our words, or, even worse than that, we might use a vulgar vocabulary.   Now, does this affects our stress level?   Yes, it has a lot to do with it.

We have learned earlier that our brain continuously forms neuron associations between video, audio, and a feeling, of any information that we come in contact with.   And all these neuron associations, are stored in our memory, for possible retrieval in the future, or for use as reference in the decision making process.

So, what kind of feelings have we attached to positive words?   Yes, positive feelings.

And, what kind of feelings have we attached to negative words?   You're right again, negative feelings.   Now, do you think that somebody must be a rocket scientist to realize, that the more negative words we use, the more negative feelings we have from the memories we retrieve?

And, by the same token, the more positive words we use, the more positive feelings we enjoy from the memories retrieved?

So, then a simple way to avoid a lot of stress is to learn to use affirmative sentences, rather than negative ones.   Instead of cursing, why not blessing, knowing that acting this way the first favor we do is ours, and then others.

See, the choice of words we use has basically almost the same effect over us, as it has over others, to whom they were intended. Can you speak in a very nice manner to somebody, and the same time feel negative? Most probably not. And can you speak in a negative, or even nasty manner to somebody, and the same time feel positive?

I don't think so.

When two or more people have an abusive exchange of words, calling each other names, how do you think all of them feel? Of course, they will feel angry and negative. Then remember, for you to avoid negative feeling and eventually stress, learn to use sentences that trigger in your mind positive feelings, and not negative ones. Using negative language, this will trigger also in the other people's mind a negative feeling, which in turn will condition them to do the same.

But if you use positive language, this will trigger in their mind a positive feeling and their reaction toward you will be positive, which in turn, will trigger a positive feeling in yourself.

It's like a circle, one feeds the other. And of course, when one feeds the other with positive words, the other is unconsciously conditioned to do the same. And also the other way around, unless one of them unconsciously, or not, breaks this cycle.

So, remember next time when you are tempted to use "politically incorrect vocabulary", that you are the first one to be affected by it.

4.   The fourth step:

POSITIVE ANCHORING.

We know, that our conscious mind can hold only one thought at the time. In other words, consciously we are able to think and concentrate, to one subject at the time.

Also, we know that based on the law of substitution, we can replace a thought with another one, a positive one with a negative, or a negative with a positive. Basically we do this every day, we are just not necessarily aware of it. Knowing this, we can learn a habit to be aware of the quality of our thoughts, and once we do not like the effect they have over us, we can willingly change them. And of course, then our state of mind changes.

We all know, that if we think positively we feel positive, but if we think negative, we feel negative. In other words, our state of mind depends on the quality of our thoughts.

We mentioned earlier, that there are two categories of people:

Ones that for some reason have the habit of seeing things through a positive mental attitude, or optimists, and others who have the habit of seeing things with a negative attitude, or pessimists.

Now, if we are persons with a positive mental attitude, good for us, but is there anything we might be able to do if we are persons with a negative mental attitude? Well, yes it is.

And as we mentioned before, the first step is to become aware of this, because unless we are aware of it, we might never develop a desire to change it.

See, our reaction to the environment, is a habitual reaction. In other words, during our life we form different habits to react in one way or the other to the environment. But we all know, habits are learned behaviors, and we can change them, if we like. So, let's see an easy way to change the habit of looking through a negative mental attitude, with a new habit of looking through a positive mental attitude. This technique we might call:

"Anchoring". There are many ways somebody might use this method, so we will use one of them.

Let's take a simple example to illustrate this.

You might remember my son Nathan. One day, few years ago he came from school upset, and with a serious tone of voice told me:

Daddy, I don't want to go to school tomorrow, I hate the school, the other kids are bothering me, so forget about it, it sucks.

Now, this was an interesting statement from a bright boy like him, but I knew that something was not right, and I had to do something about it. So after he finished his statement, I approached him, and with a nice tone of voice I said:

So, you surely had a bad day at school today, ha?

Of course I did, he answers, glad that he is not alone in his opinion. You know, Nathan, there are sunny days, and also rainy days, don't you?

But should I stay home, because it rains outside? Or should I get an umbrella, to protect myself from the rain, what do you think I should do Nathan?

Go, to work daddy, we need the money, he tells me. But I don't feel like I should go, Nathan. Daddy, I know that you should go.

You're right about that, Nathan. But how come you know that Nathan?

Because I am a smart boy, that's why. He answers me.

Well how come you are so smart? You must like to learn to be that smart, don't you?

Of course, and I can get even smarter.

I believe you, and surely know you appreciate the value of learning. They made the school for this purpose, and you won't let a little rain stops you from becoming smarter and wiser, will you Nathan?

You're right daddy he said.

So, to make a long story short he got the point, and even more than that his grades really improved.

Now, what have I done here?

First, I recognized the way he saw the situation, which puts me on his side, as a friend who understands him.

Second, I helped him to see that there is difference between our whole life, and an incident.

Third, I found something that is valuable to him, and helped him recognize that.

Fourth, I anchored the new habit, or idea, to that something which is valuable to him, and emphasized the connection between the two.

Fifth, once he gets the point, I make sure that I will remind him, as often as it might be needed, about the advantages he gets by doing that.

See, this technique is not something new we basically use it many times without being aware of it.

And as a matter of fact, by wrongly using it, we are creating much of the stress that we encounter.

Let's take another example to illustrate this point.

For many people their job has become a source of stress. And for them, going to work means to expose themselves to a stressful environment.

Now how come anchoring might be responsible for this.

Remember, I said wrongly used, it might be responsible for causing stress. So, is our negligence, or misunderstanding that is the root of it, not the method itself.

Going back to our example with the job let me ask you a simple question:

Was the job always stressful for them?

The answer is: No.

There was a time, when they were anxiously waiting to go to work, so they could get paid and buy those things they really wanted. But in time, something happened. The economical situation started to deteriorate, the prices went high, bills started pilling up, so the same amount of money was not enough to cover all the expenses. Instead of appreciating the job the same as before, they start little by little to anchor all these negative feeling to the job, because they were not making enough money. The truth of the matter is, that by having the job, they still manage at least part of the expenses, and it should not be blamed for the difficult situations they are going through.

But by doing that, any time they think about their job, it becomes a stress or for them.

Basically, the same thing happens with all the so called "stress ors". They become stress ors after that person starts to go through difficult situations and unconsciously they started to anchor, or associate negative feeling to these so called stress ors.

So, the solution is to do exactly the opposite. Remove these negative anchors, and replace them with positive ones, and the stress disappears by itself. We can use this method in conjunction with others, or just with ourselves.

Let's take a simple example:

Suppose that you are overweight, and would like to loose some weight. You might fall for, one or more of these weight loss programs, and get the best out of them, or you could do a simple anchoring here, and the results will be much better.

See, people are over weight, for two basic reasons beside genetic factors:

One, is they eat too much, and the other, they eat unhealthy foods.

So, first you anchor in your mind the word food with the word healthy, and you keep repeating to yourself till it becomes a habit: I like healthy foods, I like healthy foods. Take a piece of paper and write 50 times, or even 100 times this sentence, till it goes into your subconscious mind, and becomes a habit. Then ask yourself this simple question:

Do I live to eat, or I eat to live?

Then, once you realize that most probably you might want to eat, to live, not live to eat, keep telling yourself this till it becomes a new habit, which in turn will be triggered by your subconscious mind, before you start eating, helping you to become a person with moderate eating habits.

So what we have done here is to anchor positive things to the ones that we might need improvement.

In other words, you are replacing the unproductive notion that overeating is bad with the productive mindset that healthy eating is good.

Remember, we learned earlier, that whatever we believe to be true, it becomes truth for us. Once we accepted this idea, pretty soon we will stop craving toward unhealthy foods, and will be attracted toward healthy ones. It's as simple as that and the results are permanent.

See, most of these weight loss programs, are not aware of the fact that overeating is triggered by a bad habit, so they do not focus in replacing the habit from its roots.

There is a very appropriate proverb that says:

"A man convinced against his will, he has his own opinion still"

The same thing happens with our subconscious mind. Even though we might try to influence its response to food, by these diet programs, unless it is convinced itself by our conscious mind, it will still trigger the old habit of overeating.

5.   The fifth step:

SCREENING.

We all know, that a filter is something that stops certain things, and lets others go through it. As we mentioned before, as long as we live, we continually absorb information from our environment, which is "stored in our memory."

Now, there is a simple question here, to ask you:

Does it make any sense, to absorb and save, damaging information in our memory, which later on when retrieved, will affect us negative?

Well I don't think so, and neither do you.

Then, shouldn't we learn a habit of screening the information that we come in contact with, from our environment? Of course we should. The favor we do is ours. Remember the saying:

"Buy American, the job you save might be yours."

So, the same thing happens when it comes to screening.

Screen the information that enters your mind, the peace of mind you might preserve, is yours.

Now, let's see how we can do that.

We mentioned earlier, that whatever we choose to believe and accept becomes truth for us, and is "stored in our memory", forming the data base for our decision taking process.

Now, is all the information that we come in contact with, good for us? Of course not. Then, it does make sense to learn how to screen the information, avoiding this way to fill up our mind with information that later on, might be stress producers. Basically, to a degree, all of us do this, and most of the time we do it unconsciously. But we need more than that we need to learn to discriminate, between normal, positive information, and potential stress producing information.

See, like in the case of our health, anything that is unhealthy, might have sooner or later, a negative effect over us. The same way, the information that we put in our memory, sooner or later, will affect us in a positive, or negative way, based on its positivity, or negativity.

So, it's important to take a serious look at the way we choose to accept, knowing that like the proverb says: "We will reap, whatever we have sown".

We are living today, in a society where money comes first, and everything is centered around the mighty dollar. So many companies, especially these in the entertainment business, use information that appeal to the senses of our inexperienced young generation, not realizing that for the moment, they enjoy the hype of violence and immorality, portrayed in their entertainment, but all these are stored in the young generation's minds, forming the data base for their future behavior. And, there is no wonder, why we see more and more violence, immorality, and depravity among our youths today. All these negative behaviors, come from somewhere, and the reality is, that they come from the information that we are letting to enter in their mind, without teaching them how to screen these. So, it's important to realize, that for ourselves, we are responsible, and we should be the ones that do something about it, by learning to stop accepting anything that honestly we don't want to materialize in our life.

Now, let's go and talk about the second ability that we posses:

Chapter 3.

1. "IMAGINATION".

We mentioned earlier, that imagination is our brain's ability, to combine any kind of information, based on specific rules, and give us the right answer, based on the quality of the information that we have combined. Knowing that, we can spare ourselves much pain, sorrow, anxiety and stress, just by the simple fact of stopping combining the information that will result in these. See, all these negative states of mind we just mentioned, come from ourselves, because unaware we keep combining wrong information, and of course that the results are negative. If you have a car that requires unleaded gasoline, and you fill it up with diesel fuel, do you think that it will work normally? Not at all. But, the truth of the matter is, that we are responsible for our thoughts and feelings; nobody else puts a gun to our head, and forces us to think this way.

Now let's see how can we eliminate these unpleasant situations, by recognizing what are these wrong combinations that we often do, resulting in these negative states:

1. Things that are unchangeable, or non solvable.

2. Things from the past.

3. Unrealistic expectations, or unfulfilled dreams.

4. Inner needs and fears.

Now, let's take one at the time, and see how we can react the right way, to these particular situations, and by doing that, we are eliminating potential stress ors.

THINGS THAT ARE UNCHANGABLE OR NON-SOLVABLE.

We all know, that during our life we go through many kinds of situations, which are causing us pain and discomfort. And our natural tendency is to find ways to eliminate these, so our life could be as pleasant as possible. And, this is a normal thing to want. The reality is, that many times we are not careful to analyze if these are in our power to change, and we may be unaware that we are working hard, to do the impossible. Sometimes we need to change our thinking, or our actions, to stop the unwanted results. And these things are the unchangeable and so non-solvable. And it is our responsibility to learn to differentiate between these, and the ones that are changeable and solvable.

> The serenity prayer
>
> God, give us the grace to accept with serenity
> The things that cannot be changed,
> Courage to change the things that should be changed.
> And the wisdom to distinguish one from another

Now, let's see who, or what these things might be, and what is the best way to deal with them, so they will be no more causes of stress for us.

Many of us, would like to change family members such as: spouse, kids, parents, and other relatives. Also beside family members we might include others such as: neighbors, friends, coworkers, strangers, enemies, and so on.

But can we change them? No, we cannot. Can we help them to change? Yes, but we have to learn how. You might remember the saying:

"The kids don't do what they were told by the parents, but what they see their parents doing" or "Monkey see, monkey do.

"So, you want to help your kids change? Do it the right way, and they will copy you.

You want them to listen to you? Start listening to them first, be interested in them, and they will start to be interested in you. The main reason that kids are not listening to their parents is that the parents might know how to be parents, but they fail to be their kid's friends.

Let me ask you a little question:

If you ask any of the kids today, no matter where they come from, with whom would they like to spend their vacation, or their free time, with their best friends, or with any other person?

And from whom they might accept any advice? From their best friends or from others?

I almost can guarantee you, that all of them will choose their best friends, over any others.

So, do you want your kids to listen to you? You learn to become their best friend.

And, once you start to do that, after a while you will see, that they start to copy you; they will become your best friend too. And do best friends listen to each other? Yes they do.

Now, beside the family members, that we might want to change, we have mentioned also neighbors, friends, coworkers, strangers, enemy, and so on. Can we change any of them?

Let's talk about the enemies. Can we change them? No, and it's useless to even try. But can we help ourselves not to be stressed by them? Yes, we can. We just have to learn how. And let's see, how can we do that.

Remember the example with rain? Well, I don't want to get wet, so because of the rain, I will stay home, and will not go to work. Right? Do any of us do that? No. We get an umbrella, and protect ourselves from rain, don't we?

Yes, and this is a normal thing to do. But let's say that instead of rain, we have to deal with some "enemies." Does it make sense, to do the same thing and instead of complaining how dangerous they are, we should look to protect ourselves?

47

It makes perfect sense. Now let's see how can we do that. The "enemies," like the rain they do their thing, and we cannot expect that they might change, because most probably they would not. Then, we take the initiative to protect ourselves. In the case of rain, we get an umbrella. How about in the case of "enemies"? Well, we learn to use a kind of "umbrella" which protects us from the "enemies" negative effect over us. Remember we are not looking to change, or to straighten them up, so they will be the way we want them to be, no, but to protect ourselves.

Now we have here two kinds of situations:

1. When the "enemies" are physically present, as individuals or situations.

2.   When the "enemies" are not present, but they are still "enemies" we have to deal with them.

Let's take the first situation.

1. When the "enemies" are present and we have to deal with them.

Now, we are referring to the "enemies", as anybody, that by interacting with, we start to get stressed. We start to become irritated and eventually stressed, not because the persons themselves, but because when we see them, our mind starts recalling from its memory, many files that contain negative feelings, that we have "stored" in the past, towards people that we consider to be our "enemies".

And these feelings, we start to relive now in the present, but unconsciously we blame it on the "enemies". But, what if we look at the "enemies" differently than before, let's say that when we see them we look at them, as we might look at a disabled person. Then guess what? Our mind will start to recall from our memory, feelings that we previously attached to a disabled person, which is a feeling of sorrow, and sympathy, and there will be no more feelings of hate, or stress, or enmity towards them. Now is this a hard thing to do? No. Did we change them? No, They are still the same persons. But, did we change our feelings toward them? Yes, we did.

You might know, that Jesus Christ, considered by many, "The Greatest man that ever lived", told his own disciples, to love their enemies. Did you ever wonder, why He would ask them to do that? Do you think he cared more about the enemies, rather than his own disciples? I don't think so. But, what he knew then, is what we are learning now. He knew the way our minds function, the way the brain absorbs and processes the information from around us, and the way this information affects our present state of mind. So, by telling them to love their enemies, basically he taught them to make positive associations in their mind about people, to see the good from them, and this way, when they have to deal with them, there are no negative associations in their memory to recall, so they might have a stressful effect over them. The only thing is, that we get used to the wrong idea, that we must hate and destroy our enemies, that's why from an young age, we start to associate negative feeling in our mind toward people that we don't like or support, and of course that any time, we interact with them we unconsciously recall these files with negativity attached to them. And as Nathan used to say:

"They made me do it" Well, as you can see now, nobody makes you do it. Unconsciously you do it to yourself, and blame it on others.

Now if we start to look at our "enemies", as some disabled persons, what kind of response do you think we might get from them? Well, to help a little bit here let's ask ourselves a simple question:

When we see an enemy, and we believe that he is our enemy, do you think that our facial expression and vocabulary might reflect it? Of course it does.

Then, how do you think that the enemy will respond to us when he sees us? In a kind, and loving manner?

No. Most probably the opposite.

Then, how we are going to respond to his response? The same way, and we start to feed each other with negative feelings, making the situation more difficult than it previously was. Now, what if without telling him, we look at him as being a victim, who not being able to function properly does something that might offend us.

What do you think he will see in our facial expression and vocabulary? And, what will be his reaction toward us? Most probably, seeing us, as a non dangerous person, his reaction will be much more positive; he sees no reason to start to defend himself, because we pose no threat for him. Having a positive reaction, we also feel no danger to defend ourselves from, and little by little the interaction with him becomes a positive instead of a negative, stress producing one. So, we can see, that if we really want to solve our stress problem, there is always a way. Remember the saying:

"Where there is a will, there is also a way".

2. When the "enemies" are not physically present, but we still have to deal with them.

Let's say, for example, that it is Friday afternoon, you just finished your work early, and are anxious to get home sooner. You have plans to go away for the weekend. And halfway home on the freeway, one mile in front of you, a major accident just happened, and you get stuck for more than one hour, till the whole mess clears up. And for many of us, this might be a very frustrating time, and probably, a source of stress. Now, there is no present enemy, but still you have a, so called "stress or". The traffic jam. What can you do about this situation? Remember, you cannot change the situation itself. But what you can change is the way you look at it. Because the way you feel, is determined by the way you see it.

Now, you can start to think negative, and see what's bad about it, and for sure you might find plenty, or, you can think positive, and see what's good about it. And, once you start to look for the positive, you will come up with positive answers.

Remember, how many times you wished to have some free time for yourself, so nobody can bother you? Now, you have more than an hour for yourself. Why not, use this time to relax and enjoy without anybody bothering you? You could use this time in making some plans, or to find a solution of some of your dealings, for which you had no time before, and you kept putting them off. See, once you have the right attitude and work on it, the mind is going to give you the necessary answers. The whole secret is to know that you have to look for the good in any situation. Learn the habit of asking yourself a simple question: "What's good about this?" And honestly try to look for an answer. And always you will come up with something good. But you will never find the good out of it, without looking for it.

So, from these examples, we could realize that by using our faculty of imagination properly, we start to combine positive information, and as a result we get a positive feeling, eliminating this way the possibility of getting stressed from some situations that are not necessarily positive.

Remember, the way you feel is not determined by the situation itself, but by the way you interpret it. So, by learning to differentiate between unchangeable and changeable, and dealing properly with the ones that we cannot control, we avoid much of the stress that otherwise we might have to encounter, when dealing with these situations.

THINGS FROM THE PAST.

Now, beside the unchangeable, that might cause us to get stressed, we have to deal with many things that are part of our past, and even though they have passed, long ago, they might have a stressful effect over us. The major reason that this happens is not because of them, but as with the others, we don't know how to deal with them properly. Not knowing how our mind works, we are confusing the past with the present, and as we mentioned before, our subconscious mind cannot differentiate between reality and fiction, we keep feeding ourselves with wrong information, which are processed by our brain, and as result is a negative state of mind, and eventually stress.

As imperfect humans, many times we made mistakes, and sometimes we repeat these mistakes maybe too often, and this might be a source of sadness, and negative feelings. Now the question is, why do we keep going back to the past, and keep thinking about it? Because finding out the answer to this question, will make it much easier to work on fixing our problem.

So, why do we keep thinking about the past?

Now, during our growing up, we learned that we should succeed in what we do, and unless we succeed, we failed. So, once we failed, we did wrong, and we must change that. We don't want to be losers, but winners.

Now, it is advisable to change when we do wrong, but the key is how do we consider when we fail?

See, the winners consider their failures as learning experiences, not to be repeated.

The loser sees failure as a setback, and gets upset when he looses, and instead of learning, he starts to blame himself or others, and he keeps doing that, and of course that he does not become a winner, but by keeping recycling the same kind of thoughts, he sets himself for failure again in the future.

The right way to learn is, by rying something after we have enough information, and seeing if it works or not. If it works, then keep repeating and improving, but if does not work, it means that we need to look for another way, or improve the old one, and try again.

Do you remember how you learned to walk? You kept falling down, but did you give up, and never got up again, thinking how incapable you were? Or every time you have fallen, you got up, again and again till after awhile, you started to be able to walk straight. See, in learning the process is the same, no matter what we need to learn. And the secret in learning is:

Have the right information, persist on it never give up, and sooner then you think, you start to master that particular; which becomes a habit.

Now, what we need to learn about the past?

First, the past is gone, and never will be back, unless we make the future, as the past was.

So, does it make any sense to want to change the past? No.

Second, is to avoid doing again, the wrong things we have done in the past, because they will bring the same negative consequences. Instead, see the good things, that we have done in the past, and keep doing them again.

Now, another thing that we need to learn about the past is that even though it is gone, our brain holds in its memory banks all the information from our past, and it uses them in our thinking process. And many times what we do is, we use our faculty of imagination and combine past information. And any time when we start to combine negative information, even though our intention might be good, we start to feel a negative state of mind, which was previously attached to this negative information that we are now combining.

So, it makes perfect sense to understand, and realize that, we don't do us any favor, by combining negative information, because we will create for ourselves a negative state of mind. It's much better to learn the habit of combining positive information from the past, and learning from them, at the same time creating for us a positive state of mind.

UNREALISTIC EXPECTATIONS OR UNFULFILLED DREAMS.

Now, the third category of causes, that might result in stress are unrealistic expectations, or unfulfilled dreams. Let's elaborate a little bit, and see what can we do about these, so they won't be anymore a source of stress.

If we go back in our childhood, we might remember that we used to have a high sense of urgency. We wanted something, and we wanted it right away. When we saw that toy, or that Barbie, we wanted it right away, not tomorrow or some other time, but right now.

Tomorrow will never come, I want it right now.

We might remember that, or we might remember when our kids did the same to us. They want it now. Now, as kids of course we didn't want everything right away, but everyone of us wanted something, that we considered to be special for us. And the truth of the matter is, we didn't get too often that special thing, so unaware of, we developed an inner craving towards some things that are still in us, even though we might be adults now.

So, that inner craving is manifested into a different way now, we might not want a toy, or a Barbie, but surely there might be other things that we have in mind. There is nothing wrong with wanting to have more than we used to, but the problem rises when, unaware of it we want something that we just cannot get now. And the same feeling of urgency, that we had when we were kids, comes over us, and because we are not able to acquire that particular thing or objective, it becomes a stress or for us. But basically, it's not the objective itself, that is stressing us, but the memory of being helpless and incapable to get it, which was "stored in our memory," and comes now in the present, and we start to feel it; that's the cause of our stress.

What we need to do is to understand this and learn to react properly, by choosing to combine positive past memories from our childhood positive experiences.

You might remember how good you felt, when you wanted something, and you got it? So, when we make plans for the future, it's wise to think about the positive past experiences, when we were able to achieve what we wanted, and use these experiences as reinforcements for our plans, instead of thinking that "most probably this won't happened, as it didn't happened in the past. We need to learn to expect positive results from us, and by doing that, based on the law of expectation little by little it will become reality.

Let me tell you a little story, from which we might learn a big lesson.

Once upon a time, like any story begins, there was a little old lady, living down the hill outside the village. Every Sunday, she had a hard time to get to the church, because she had to walk over the hill to get there. So, one Sunday morning, the priest was talking about faith, saying that if anybody would have faith, and will tell the mountain to move away, the mountain will move.

Excited to find the solution to her problem, the little old lady, after the sermon was over, went to the priest and asked him:

Do you honestly believe that this might be possible? She said.

Yes the priest answers.

Well then, it will be a piece of cake for this hill to move away, don't you think, priest? Because I always have a hard time to walk all the way over it, to get here

Yes he said. So, happily the lady starts to walk back home. But walking over the hill, she starts to doubt that it might be possible. This hill was here before she was born; where this huge hill might go? All these kind of thoughts were going through here mind, but if the priest said so, it must be true. So, once she gets home, she started to pray for the hill to move away. The very next day, she wakes up early as usual, goes to the window, and guess what? The hill is still there.

Well, I need to pray more she tells herself, so she started to pray again. Next morning, the same thing happens, the hill is still there.

One more time she said, since the priest said it is true, maybe I didn't pray enough. So, she started praying again.

Next morning, she gets up again goes at the window and look:

The hill is still there. She shacked her head and said:

I knew it, from the beginning that it won't move, and I was right about it.

Well, if we expect for our plans to become reality, like this little old lady, then we get the same results. But, we might learn to expect the good instead the bad, because as Shakespeare said:

"The fragrance of the rose, lingers in the hand that casts it"

So, our state of mind is the result of the kind of information we want to combine through our faculty of imagination. We want a positive state of mind? Then we combine positive information.

Be selective in whatever your mind ponders upon, because you are the one that has to reap whatever you are sowing.

INNER NEEDS AND FEARS

Now the last, but not the least category of possible stress ors, are the inner needs, and inner fears. We mentioned before, that in the decision making process, there are two factors that are always considered by our brain: Is the information or event producing pleasure, or it is producing pain? If it produces pleasure, it automatically is accepted by our mind, and we unconsciously attach a positive meaning to it. If it is interpreted as pain, is automatically rejected by our mind, and we attach a negative feeling to it. The more information is interpreted as positive, the more positive feeling we attach to it, and it becomes an inner need. By the same token, the more negative feeling we attach to it, it becomes an inner fear.

Now, there are two kinds of inner needs and inner fears.

1. One kind of fear or need is produced by our interaction with the environment, and is caused by the fact that we basically see things, and we begin to perceive them as positive or negative.

2. The other kind is produced by our characteristics, and qualities of our personality.

The first one depends on the way we decide to interpret the environment.

The second depends how the environment fits and matches our personality type. There is a strong relationship between the environment, and our personality that influences our behavior. In other words, each individual learns to adapt, build, or change the personality type, based on the way he interprets the quality of environment that surrounds him.

Now, let's see how come that we have these inner needs and fears, and by knowing that, we could much easier understand how to eliminate the stress that they might produce.

All of us are familiar with cars. We know that they were designed for positive purpose, to make our life easy and more

57

enjoyable. Now, cars have two distinctive attributes that are opposite to each other.

One is a mechanism that helps the car to go forward and move, so we can drive it any place we might want.

And the second, they have another mechanism, or system that helps to slow down and stop the car, so we can protect ourselves and the car in case of a difficult situation, or when is required by the situation.

Now, both of these mechanisms are good and necessary, but if they are used in a wrong way they could do much damage to us or to themselves. None of us will step hard on the brakes for no reason, at 70 miles/ hour. Why? Because we might put ourselves in a dangerous situation.

Also, we will not drive 80 miles/ hour in a 40 miles speed limit, because we don't want to cause an accident, or get a ticket. So, my point is that when used properly, the car functions properly, the way it was designed. But if for some reason, it is not used properly, these two mechanisms might become a source of pain and destruction. Now, in case that this will happen, should we blame the car, or does the responsibility fall on the driver?

The reality is that the driver is at fault, and it does not do any good to blame the car as being responsible for the damages.

The best thing to do is to work on the real source of the problem, instead of looking for something, or somebody to blame.

Now, if we look at our body, we can say that, as in case of a car, we are equipped with two mechanisms.

A. One, to identify, explore, absorb, understand and enjoy the environment.

B. And the other, that serves as protection, so we might not get hurt, when we interact with the environment.

The two mechanisms

The first one, we might call:
"THE PROPULSION MECHANISM".

The second, we might call:
"THE SELF DEFENSE MECHANISM".

As in the example with the car, if these two are used properly, our interaction with the environment is an enjoyable one. But if they are improperly used, the results might have a stressful affect over us. So, these inner needs and fears are nothing else but the manifestations of these two mechanisms, which are functioning in our bodies.

And the more we know how they work, the easier it will be to use them properly; the less we know, the more we expose ourselves to possible danger situations.

Let's take one at the time, and see how can we eliminate the stress that those might produce.

Chapter 4.

A. THE "PROPULSION MECHANISM"

As we mentioned before, the role of this mechanism is: to identify, explore, absorb, understand and enjoy the environment. Now, this mechanism is characteristic to all human beings; we all are equipped with it. Even though we all have the same mechanism, which works based on the same principle, still our reaction with the environment differs from one to the other.

And the big question is why? Well, if we study the humans at a global scale, we can realize that, the whole mankind, we might divide in four basic personality types:

1. Analytic personality.

2. Adaptive personality.

3. 3 Aggressive personality.

4. Apathetic personality.

Now, the question is: Where do all these personality types come from?

And this is a very good question, that we need to answer, and by doing that we might understand why some people's behavior differs from the others, under the same circumstances.

Now, we might approach this subject from a naive standpoint, and believe that, we just happen to be the way we are, and as the science advances, we discover many more interesting things about ourselves. But, if we really are interested in the truth, then we just cannot ignore facts that point toward different directions.

Let's go back to the example with the car. Now if you open the hood of your car, and ask many people if they could name ten different parts that are assembled under the hood, how many of them do you think could do that? Then, bring a mechanic with ten or twenty years experience in cars and see how many

61

parts he could identify? For sure more than ten. Why is that? Because the mechanic has learned and convinced himself, that he has to know all of these, what they are, how they work, and how to replace them when something goes wrong.

But to the others, who have no idea about mechanics, all these sophisticated pieces of machinery, that make the car to function properly, have no significance. They know to get in the car, turn the ignition on, and drive. The rest is the mechanic's job.

Now, does the fact that somebody is more or less aware of the way a car was designed to function, make the car something that just happened to be like that? Or, that, the car is a design for a purpose, and should be treated as such? I don't think that any of us, when we might have a problem with the car, just open the hood and look around, take some parts and throw them in, close the hood, and the repair is done. Nobody does that. We take it to the mechanic, find the diagnosis, and repair or replace the right parts that are needed.

Now, going back to our subject about we as humans, what is going to be the reaction when people hear about: brain, heart, kidneys, eyes, ears, nervous system, cardiovascular system, respiratory system, and many of our body components?

Well, depends whom you ask. If you ask common people, they will agree that they have heard about some of these, and they are part of our life. But if you ask professionals in the medical field, they will tell you, that these are very sophisticated organs and functions of our body, that work based on specific laws and principles, that we should pay attention to, because the more we respect these, the easier we make our life.

On the other hand, the more ignorant we are about them, the more miserable we might make our present and future.

Now, we ask the same question, as we did about the cars:

Does the fact that people today are more or less aware of the way that our body was designed to function, means that our body just happens to be like that? Or do we need to recognize a designer behind these sophisticated systems and functions?

See, my friend, ignorance is not going to change the real truth.

Now, we can decide to accept the idea that we just happened to be what we are. Or, be more realistic, and recognize that we are a design of a powerful, and loving Designer.

Because the truth of the matter is, that this is what we are:

An intelligent design, by an intelligent Designer.

We know, that by understanding the purpose of a design, it's much easier to understand how it functions, because always there must be a relationship between the purpose of the product, and the way it functions.

So, the best thing to do is to find out the purpose of our design, and knowing that, it will be much easier to understand the way we function. Now, what this has to do with the four personality types? Well, if we look around us, to the way the " Nature" is working, we can safely say, that there are four major characteristics or attributes that are involved: Power, Wisdom, Justice and Love.

For somebody to be able to set up the whole universe, with all its billions of stars and galaxies, and have a harmonious interaction between themselves, that One must be powerful. Must have a lot of power. Not only powerful, but also intelligent, to have the knowledge to do that. To know to set up all the laws that governs the universe. And coming down to our micro universe, to know how to set up all the systems that govern the functioning of our body, and also of the any other living creature that exists on the earth today.

Beside the power and wisdom, we can clearly see, that in everything around us there is a perfect balance of justice. I am not talking about human justice, which is, we could say "selective or relative justice".

We can easily recognize that the whole universe works as a unit. The earth also works like a unit, the whole of nature is harmonized in such a way, that everything is in its place, and functions the way it is supposed to.

Now, the fourth and maybe the most important attribute, is love. Why is that? Because the purpose of the whole universe to function the way it does is to maintain a perfect balance on the earth, so we humans might live a joyful life. Only we humans, have the capacity of understanding, and enjoying the environment. No other creature on the earth today, is equipped with this faculty. All the others were designed to contribute to our joyful life.

Going back to the four personality types, we as humans were equipped with these four attributes: Power, wisdom, justice and love. We all manifest these qualities in our life, but for some reason, because we are less than perfect, many times we use them improperly, or in the wrong situation, and as result, among other negative outcome, we might have to put up with stress. Out of these four qualities, derived the four personality types. And no matter who we are, or where we come from, we use them daily. As we mentioned before, we are less than perfect, and many times we just don't know how to react, and we are just doing a kind of guesswork. And of course, many times we might not like the outcome.

So, it makes perfect sense to learn to use in the right way these "attributes," and by our doing so, our life will become enjoyable, and also it will be free of stress.

Now, let's go back to the inner needs and fears, and see how can we eliminate the stress that might be produced by them.

One important thing that we need to know is what kind of personality type is predominant in our lives. This is important, because we interpret any information that comes from the environment, based on our particular personality type. Once we honestly found out which one is predominant in us, the next step is to find out as soon as possible, what kind of personality type are the persons we are mostly dealing with. Knowing that, we realize that everyone has some specific needs and fears. If we want our interaction with them to be positive, then we make sure that we do our utmost to meet their needs, and avoid feeding their fears. Doing that, we are eliminating a wide range of possible stress ors.

64

Let's see now what are some of the needs and fears of these four personality types.

1. Analytic personality type.

These are people with above average thinking ability. They like to go in details, and use precise information. If somebody asks you what time is it? And you say it's about noon, they will say: No, it's eleven fifty eight and a half. And they are probably right. Now their basic fears are insufficient information.

So when you have to deal with these kinds of people, it is important to keep in mind what they want, and what they fear.

2. Adaptive personality type.

These are warm and kind people that we might call: " people pleasers" because they have a need to please others. They adapt themselves to many situations to be able to please others. They feel good to help, and care for others. Another reason they do that is, that they have a deep fear of rejection. They want to be accepted, and not rejected, so they will go out of their way, to please everybody. A side effect of this personality type is, that many times, they set themselves for failure by trying to please everybody, and not being able to do so all the time.

3. Aggressive personality type.

Opposite to the adaptive type, the aggressive have the need to be pleased, to control, direct and advise others, to know everything, to have always the last word in a conversation. In other words, they need to be in power and control of the events and other people they are dealing with. They will stop at nothing, to fill this inner need. Their major fear is, to be in subjection to others, or to listen to their advice. You do not teach an aggressive, rather he wants to teach you, even though he might not be qualified to do so.

4. Apathetic personality type.

Now, if the aggressive ones want to know everything, the apathetic ones, are exactly the opposite. They rather stay away, and not getting involved in anything. We might call them: "The loners". They have a deep fear of involvement.

Knowing that people we are dealing with have these needs and fears, based on their individual type, we can easily avoid confrontation and stress, by doing our best in meeting their needs, instead of feeding their fears. Also we need to keep in mind, that every event or situation is interpreted by each individual, based on his or hers own personality type.

Let's go back to the example with the traffic jam to illustrate this.

Now, if you were an analytic personality type, how do you think you might react when you find out that you are stuck, for more than an hour in the traffic? Being an analytic type, most probably you might use this time to plan all the details you might need for the weekend.

As an adaptive type, you might start to be concerned about the well being of the people involved in the accident, and you might even try to get of the car, and go to the accident site, to see if you might be of help. Also you might be worried about your family, they are preparing alone for the weekend, and you are not there to help them.

Well, being an aggressive type, your first reaction might be: What's going on here? What's wrong with these people, don't they know how to drive?

I have important things to do this weekend, Can't they see that? I don't know why they give driver license to anybody, so they could cause accidents and inconvenience others? And so on.

Now, if you were an apathetic type, most probably don't care too much about what just happened. As long as it does not bother you, you might find a way to kill this time and get over it

Now, when we deal with a situation, it's much easier than when we deal with people. The situation is the same for everybody, its meaning changes when individuals interpret it in different ways. But, if we have to deal with people, then we need to be even more careful, because aside interpreting the situation according to our understanding, based on our personality type, they also give the meaning to the situation, based on their personality type. And as we mentioned before, everyone wants his own needs to be met. Many times, this causes a difficult situation, and most of the time, results in stress. Then, how can we avoid that?

Well, the secret is, that no matter how strong our needs or fears are, we have the power to control them. The only thing is that we are not aware of that. Once we become aware of this important fact, then we start to learn how to control the situation.

First, it might seem that is impossible to do, and we might fail, but if we really want it, actually is much easier than it might seem to be. It's just a matter of forming new and healthy habits, and getting rid of some others, that are causing us stress.

Now, all these four personality types that we might posses are very good, and we need them. The problem rises, when we do not know when to use the right one. We need to learn which of these we should use in a particular situation, and which ones to avoid. Because we just cannot expect to react any way we want, and also get the results we want. We do not live in a perfect world yet. So we need to learn to be selective.

Now understanding these facts, let's go back to the propulsion mechanism.

As we mentioned before, it was designed to identify, explore, absorb, understand and enjoy the environment. Knowing that each of us has his own personality type, then it make perfect sense to keep in mind that the negative outcomes, or stressful situations that we many times encounter, are nothing else but misrepresentations of the reality of events.

Even though the line of communication between us and the events, or other people might be open, they are caused by the fact that everybody has a different opinion about them, based on each individual personality type. So, the solution is very simple; accept the reality that each individual has this mechanism of propulsion which continuously pushes him or her to interact with the environment. Then, realize that the meaning that each gives to the environment is dictated by the way he understands it, which might differ from ours. And the decisions he is making are not based on our understanding of the environment, but his. Also, each individual, unaware of, puts his own needs first, and then the others, and of course when everybody does that, somebody might not get his needs met. Not all the athletes who run for a race might get the first place. Understanding these realities of life, we might learn to synchronize these four attributes that we posses, in such a way that we might get the desired outcome for ourselves, and for other also. Professionals call this self-actualization.

People forget that we as humans are basically only one family, and in our fight to survive, we sacrifice each other to obtain what we think we might want. And many times after we got what we thought we wanted, we realized that was not the desired outcome. Instead of learning from our mistakes, we keep going with stronger motivation, chasing another goal that seems to be more satisfying.

Unaware, we might cause more pain and sorrow, to ourselves and others, even though our intentions we perceived as good.

But, by understanding the way we function, we might keep in mind that we all have the right to be happy, and there is a way to do that. Is just a matter of finding it, and applying its principles.

Chapter 5.

B. THE "SELF-DEFENSE MECHANISM"

Now, for us to be able to really explore and enjoy the environment, we were equipped also with this self defense mechanism. Its role is to prevent us from possible injury or even death. Let's see how this works: If we take a closer look at our brain, we can safely say, that it works on two levels:

1.   Subconscious level.

2.   Conscious level.

Let's take one at the time, and see how these work:

1. THE SUBCONSCIOUS LEVEL

We know, that all of us are equipped with a so call "Nervous system", which is designed to alert us about anything that might present a danger for our body. And the way it does that, is through the feeling of pain. We mentioned before, that as humans we were designed to enjoy the environment we live in. So, anytime our senses detect any possible dangers, the nervous system goes on alert.

Based on the level of perceived danger, it triggers a certain level of pain.

Now, the subconscious level works based on two kinds of information:

A.   Inner information, that has to do with our body's components.

B.   Outer information, that has to do with the information received from outside of our body, in other words, from the environment.

Now, let's take one at the time, and see how they work.

A. Inner information.

We know, that our body is made up of a number of organs, that all contribute to our normal functionality as humans. Also we know, that each of these has a special role to play and all have to work in harmony, so the whole body might function properly.

Many times, we might remember that we have experienced different kinds of pain. Sometimes we might have gotten a headache, or chest pain, or back pain, or something else. All these feelings of pain are nothing else but warning signals from our nervous system, that something is not right, or does not function properly in that specific area, where the feelings of pain came from. And we should pay attention, and do something about them.

70

The mistake we make is, that many times, we use painkillers, which are doing nothing else, but numb the pain, while the cause of pain is still there.

Remember on your car, if you look on the dashboard you see many gages and indicators. Also you might see some red lights that might flash some time. Suppose you are driving your car, then suddenly a red light goes on, and when you look closely, you see that this is the oil light. Would you stop the car and check the oil level, to make sure that is O.K. or you take some masking tape, and tape over the light so it won't bother you anymore?

Well, obviously you will be smart enough to stop and check the car, instead of covering the light. But, it might surprise you to find out, that every time somebody uses painkiller, without trying to find out the cause of their pain, they are doing nothing else, but covering the light. By doing this, they will cause the problem to get bigger, instead of eliminating it.

So, the subconscious level of the nervous system goes in alert any time it perceives that one of its body components might not function properly, and a conscious decision needs to be taken.

B. Outer information.

Now, beside the information received from our own body components, the subconscious level works also with the information received from the environment. To illustrate this, let me ask you few simple questions: When do you eat, or should eat? When do you drink? Why don't you use the same wardrobe in the summer, as in the winter? Why do you sneeze? Or why do you wear sunglasses? We all do these things, and are familiar with them. But did it ever cross your mind, why we do these things? The answer is that our subconscious level of the protective mechanism based on the information collected from the environment, triggers these actions for our protection. When we feel hungry, or thirsty, that is the warning that our body needs to assimilate food to maintain its proper functionality.

71

When the temperature changes, the same thing happens, we are warned by the feeling of cold or heat that we need to take an action.

Now, if we obey right away these warnings, things are going to be fine, but if we keep ignoring, or overreacting to them, two things might happen:

1. The warning signals become more accentuated, till we do something about them.
2. We might alter our response to the environment into a positive, or negative way.

Now, in the first case, the worst that might happen, is that we might require medical attention to be able to resolve the situation.

But, in the second case, if we alter our response to the information from the environment, this might be a major source of stress, when we do it in a negative way.

We might know people who get scared very fast, and many small things are major challenges, or problems for them. They have this so called quality "to major in minor things", when it comes to their reaction towards these events. Also you might know some, who have the habit of saying:

Don't worry, nothing bad could happen. But soon after that they have to suffer the consequences of their negligence.

These people, have unconsciously altered their proper response to the environment in a negative way, and many times for them, this might becomes a source of stress.

So, as we have seen from this information, the subconscious level of our protective mechanism goes on alert, and if it is not properly understood, it might be considered as a source of stress. But, the reality is that it's just doing the job for which it was designed. We are the ones that by not knowing misunderstand its functionality.

Now, let's go further and see how the conscious level of our defense mechanism works, and how it might help us to eliminate many potential stress ors.

2. THE CONSCIOUS LEVEL

Beside the subconscious level, which reacts to the environment without our conscious awareness, our defense mechanism goes on alert also when is triggered by its conscious level.

Let's use an example to illustrate this.

Suppose that you just bought a new car, a nice sporty car. One day, coming back from work, just before you get into the freeway, one of your high school friends passes you by, and right when he is side by side, tells you:

Hey John, you got a new car, but you are still slower than me. Let's see if you can catch up with me, and he speeds up in the freeway.

Now, this incident might bring you past memories about your adventures during the high school years, and the tendency is to go for it. But now, that time has gone, and who's first is not so important for you anymore.

And because you start thinking about the potential negative consequences that an action like this might have, you decide to control yourself. Your safety is more important than a game.

This is a simple example, from which we could see how the conscious level of our defense mechanism works. Basically we consciously use this level every day, with any information that comes from environment. We have learned earlier that any decision we might take is based on two questions that consciously or not we ask ourselves: Does this bring me pleasure, or it is going to bring me pain? And these questions are the work of the conscious level of our protective mechanism. Now there is a very important question that we need to ask here:

What is the standard used for comparison when we take a decision, to identify something as good or bad?

Well, let's take an example to illustrate this:

Suppose that, there is a family of emigrants coming to America from, let's say China. We have two parents, and four little kids. But when they came here, for some reason, only two kids came with them, and the other two remained there, with their grand parents. They were two and three years old. The

73

ones that came to the US is four and five years old. Now all were born in China, and started to learn the Chinese language and customs. But what do you think is going to happen after ten or twenty years? Well, the ones that came here, even though they were born the same place as the other two, will change completely. They will speak a totally different language their customs also might be different than those of the Chinese people.

Why does this happen?

Because, when we are born our brain is like a huge and empty library. Soon after we were born, we start to fill up this library with all the information that we, consciously or not, absorb from the environment. We might think that the past is gone, but this is true only for the conscious mind. But for the subconscious mind, there is no such thing as past, present or future. Each bit of information that entered in it is still there, and ready to be retrieved when is asked for. We might not know how to retrieve it, but it's still there. And all the information that we have absorbed during our entire life becomes the database for our thinking process.

So, to answer our question that we asked ourselves earlier, we can say that: All the decisions that we take concerning the conscious level of our defensive mechanism are made based on all previous information that are contained in our subconscious mind, about that particular subject. How this could be? Well, first we should know that there is a relationship between the conscious level and subconscious level.

Anytime when we talk or ask ourselves any questions, we are sending a signal to the subconscious mind to find the answer to our question.

And, soon after that a thought comes in our mind, which is the answer from our subconscious level. Now, many times we get a negative or wrong answer, you might say: Why is that?

Well, there is a simple explanation to that.

We have asked ourselves wrong questions. That's why we get unpleasant answers.

Remember, the subconscious mind does not pass any judgment over the information it receives as good or bad. It accepts it as truth as long as the conscious mind does so. That's

74

why even though all four kids from our example, were born by the same parents in the same place, after ten or twenty years, they will be totally different people. Two of them, will speak and behave like Chinese people, and the other two, will speak and behave like Americans.

Now, what has this to do with stress? Well, here is the secret.

We all grew up believing that there is no solution for eliminating stress. Learning that and believing it, what will be our attitude about stress? We must live with it. So, all our conscious decisions we have made in the past reflect our thinking. What we need to do is to" come to America", so to speak. Like the two kids that came to US with their parents, they had to learn new language and new behaviors, if they really wanted to integrate themselves into this new society. The same thing happens with us. We want to eliminate stress? It's just impossible to do so with our old "language". We need to know the new one, and then we might be able to practice it. It's simple as that.

So, up till now we have learned that, our brain, as central command of our body, functions based on two mechanisms.

One "The propulsion", that helps us to identify, explore, absorb, understand and enjoy the environment.

The other, designed for our protection we have called: "The defense Mechanism" Both of these mechanisms, continuously work together in finding the right solution to the information that we get by interacting with the environment. And, as we mentioned before, they use the previous information "stored" in the memory banks as reference in any of the decisions that they make. Now, how many people are aware of this, so they learn how to use them properly, and have the desired results?

The reality is that our parents didn't know, because their parents also didn't know. They have done whatever they thought was good, which was not necessarily the best thing every time.

So, like they did, we are probably trying our best.

But, as the twelve years old kid from our example, we might "wreck the car" not necessarily because we are bad people, but just because we do not know how to properly use it. The good news is, that we all can learn the proper way. Once we understand how these two mechanisms work, then we will be smart enough to use them in such a way that they will complement each other, instead of misusing them, and as a result we get stressed.

Let's say that you buy an expensive and complicated computer, or other piece of electronic machinery. Now, without the owner's manual, it is very difficult, maybe even impossible, to operate it. But if the company that sells you the product gives you the right manual, is just a matter of applying the rules and regulations shown by the book, and everything becomes possible. The machine works well. The same thing happens with us. Once we know ourselves, the way we were designed to work, and how these two mechanisms work, it just a matter of wanting to follow the instructions.

See, all the stress that we have to face daily, is caused by the improper use of these two mechanisms.

Imagine how easy it might be for your car to go forward if you keep stepping on the brakes, or your emergency brake is on all the time? There is a lot of stress on the whole car, if it has to run like that. And this is what we basically do many times, when we unconsciously trigger the defense mechanism at the wrong time, and of course then we have no success in going forward. Consciously, we might want to go forward, but subconsciously we trigger the defense mechanism, and want to stop. The result is what we call stress.

Do you still want to live your life, as a stressful one? Then keep doing what you were doing. But if you want a life free of stress, then the solution is simple. Learn these simple things about yourself, and then apply them daily, till they become a habit. Once they are habits, you will do them as a normal thing.

Remember: "If it is to be, it's up to me". For me, I need to do it, and for you, the only one that can do it, is yourself.

So, up till now we have learned that through the ability of reasoning, we can differentiate between the information that we receive from the environment. And we have a conscious choice over the information that we are dealing with. So we can discriminate between the ones that we might want to accept, or reject. Then through the ability of imagination, we have the capacity to combine the information that we have chosen in such a way that we might get the desired results.

Now let's see how we can use the ability of manifesting emotions, might help us to make these results last. So, let's go to the next ability we posses, which is Emotion.

Chapter 6.

3. "EMOTION".

What is emotion? Well, there might be many explanations, and some might be better than others. Before we give any definition to it let's talk a little bit about a different subject that will help us better understand what emotion is. If we take a closer look at our planet we can see that life is perpetuating at different levels. What do I mean by this?

Well, we have different forms of life that exist and live on the earth.

Let's briefly cover three of these forms:

1. **Alive, unconscious, and stationary.**

2. **Alive, semiconscious, and mobile.**

3. **Alive, conscious, and mobile.**

Now let's take one at a time and see how this would help us to better understand what emotion is.

1. Alive, unconscious and stationary.

These are the huge variety of life forms that, even though are alive, they are not conscious of themselves or the environment that surrounds them. They are also stationary for the fact that their genetic make up were designed to keep them rotted to the ground. Some of these are: flowers, trees, every kinds of vegetation that we all see covering the earth today. They are alive, but being unconscious of themselves, they do not have the ability to understand or to pass a judgment on the environment that surrounds them.

2. Alive, semiconscious, and mobile.

These are the huge variety of life forms that are alive, but they are semiconscious, and have the capacity to move from one place to another, or even migrate.

We call them semiconscious because, even though they are alive, their reaction to the environment is not a conscious one, but it is based on their instinct that is like a built in program that controls their behavior. And their reaction is limited to that specific program. Some of these are: the large variety of species of animals, birds, fish, and other creatures that can move and live on earth today.

1. Alive, conscious, and mobile.

You might guess who's next by now. Yes, we are, the human specie. We are alive, have the ability to move from one place to the other, moreover, we have the ability to consciously react or respond to the environment. This ability makes us superior to any other creature on earth today. Not only able to consciously react to the environment, but have the ability to feel the enjoyment through what we call emotion. This is done through our nervous system that brings to our conscious awareness about these feelings of emotion. All other forms of life do not possess this ability of being aware of the environment, to feel it, enjoy it, be happy about it. We mentioned before, that through reasoning we consciously or unconsciously, absorb information from the environment, and through the process of imagination the brain combines them, and as a result the nervous system is activated to create a specific feeling in our body which we call emotion. In other words we are aware of the cake, we see it, we are able to taste it, enjoy it, and are able to express and share that joy.

Now let's go back to our subject of emotion.

As a third link in our three piece of chain, emotion is basically flavor of our life. We could have been designed without it and still alive and conscious, but looks like the Master Designer had more in mind about human race than to just be alive. And our ability to feel emotion proves that.

Now, somebody might ask; why then do we have to deal with negative emotions and why are they part of our life?

Well, that simple. We learned earlier that we were equipped with the two mechanisms, the propulsion and the defense mechanisms.

Through the propulsion mechanism we are pushed forward to identify, explore, absorb and enjoy the environment. As a result we feel positive emotions and thus we are happy and enjoy life. But when there is a potential or a real danger, the defense mechanism takes over and through different degree of pain (which is nothing other than negative emotions) makes us aware of the necessity of doing something about it. That's a normal thing. Now the question comes; How about stress and depression or any other negative emotions that we feel even though there is not any danger? Well, the answer to this is that feelings of stress or other negative emotions are the result of triggering the defense mechanism when actually it is not needed. This occurs because we are not aware how our mind works. When we feed our mind with positive thoughts, the subconscious part of our brain understands that everything is OK and we can enjoy whatever we are doing.

But by the same token, when we feed our mind with negative thoughts, the subconscious part of our brain understands that we are in danger and triggers the defense mechanism creating a negative emotion in our body.

It's like when you get in your car to go some place and try to drive your car with the emergency brakes on. The car might move, but there is a lot of stress on the engine and transmission.

Even though the general idea is that emotion is something that we have no control over, the truth of the matter is that, we have the power to control the intensity of this feeling we call emotion. We need just to learn how.

Remember, emotion is the result of combined information selected through reasoning. So, having a choice in selecting the information we want, we could become smart enough to select and accept information that results in desired emotions, and not into undesired ones.

The only time when we cannot control the intensity of our emotions is when the emotions are triggered by the subconscious level of defensive mechanism, when an imminent danger was perceived by it. Let's take an example to illustrate this:

Suppose you are on the sidewalk and want to cross the street. Before crossing the street, as usual you look around to make sure it's safe to do that, and then you proceed. By the time you get to the middle of the street, suddenly you hear a loud noise coming from two cars crashing together, right behind you.

Instantly your whole body goes through a state of intense emotion, your adrenaline level goes up to the roof, and most probably you get scared to death, thinking for the moment that your life is in danger, even though the accident had nothing to do with you.

Why did this happen? We mentioned before, that the defense mechanism goes on as soon as it perceives a possible danger situation, from the information that constantly absorbed from the environment.

And the crashing sound was identified as a possible danger, so it triggered the proper response; become instantly alert and find the fastest way to get out of danger, by looking toward the place the sound came from and take the necessary steps to avoid any injury. But, once you looked behind you, and saw that there were two cars involved in an accident, the high level of emotion drops drastically, and soon you get back to normal, even though that experience remains in your memory banks.

Now, these kinds of situations should not be confused with stressful situations. It does not matter how high the intensity of these kinds of emotions might be, they are not affecting our stress level, they are just a response to a perceived danger. In other words the defensive mechanism is just doing its job. The problem is, that most of the people do not know this fact, and unaware of this difference, they start to consciously attach a negative meaning to a situation like this, and by doing that, many of these kind of situations might become a source of stress for them. We might know people that get scared very easily.

For them, right away the sky is falling, even though, there might not be a real danger at all.

So, it's important to acknowledge that there is a difference between a conscious negative meaning we might give to a situation, and a proper response of the defense mechanism, when it perceives a potential danger.

The more we learn about our marvelous brain and the way it functions the easier will be for us to use it for our own benefit and eliminate negative emotions that destroying the happiness of millions of people today.

We know that there are billions of dollars spent today, to find out if there is life in other parts of the universe. This implies that the faculty of reasoning could be used to discover the wonders of the universe. So the same ability could be used to discover the wonders of our personal inner universe. And of course that the benefits could be more appreciated by those who need to solve their own inner problems.

It makes perfect sense for us as individuals, to open our eyes and recognize that we need to learn about ourselves, and our destiny. As we all know, each of us is interested primarily in his own welfare first, and them on the others.

It does not matter how good others are doing, if we are miserable and in need. Or how much peace of mind others might have, if we are missing it. Let's see now what are some expressions of this faculty of emotion.

Well, basically there are two kinds:

1. Ones, that have their roots in a positive reasoning, and are expressed in a positive way.

2. The others, that have their roots in a negative, or absence of reasoning, and of course that these are expressed, in a negative way.

Let's take one at the time:

1. POSITIVE EMOTIONS.

As we just mentioned, these emotions have their roots in a positive reasoning, and they might be, love, kindness, happiness, joy, laughter, excitement, and so on. The people who manifest these qualities, aware or not, are repeatedly using their positive reasoning towards themselves or others; till they become habits that are triggered instantly, once they are formed. So, we have a choice to use a positive reasoning, knowing that this will result in a positive emotion, which of course is what we ultimately want.

Now, let's go to the other kind of emotion, that we many times experience, negative emotion.

2. NEGATIVE EMOTIONS.

Now, if the positive emotions have their roots in positive reasoning, then based on the same law, the negative emotions have their roots in negative reasoning. Like the positive emotions, the negative ones also could be short term, or long term. Do any of us like these kinds of emotions? Of course not. Then let's see how can we identify them, and what we can do to eliminate them.

Living in our world today, many of us are facing difficult situations, and as a result we start to feel a large variety of these negative emotions. Many of us are familiar with: anxiety, depression, anger, aggression, irritation, impatience, hostility, stress and many others.

Now, what are all these? They are nothing else, but different degree of negative emotions. And as we mentioned before, they could be short term, such as: anxiety, anger, aggression, irritation, impatience, hostility, or long term such as sadness, depression and stress. Even though some might differ from others in intensity or symptoms, all of these have their roots in a negative reasoning, and of course, then we experience them as unpleasant feelings.

We might follow today's tradition and treat each of them individually, using the existent means, or recognize their common source and deal directly with it. As a result all the symptoms will disappear. Let's take an example to illustrate this:

Suppose you have a tree in your back yard that you want to get rid of. What will you do? Will you keep cutting down the branches one by one, and by the time you get finished, they might start to grow again? Or the best thing is to cut its roots, and then the whole tree withers and dies.

Well, the answer is simple. Go for the roots. The same thing happens with these negative emotions that we have to deal with. Instead of spending our time trying to deal with one at the time, it's better to find their roots and work there.

Then, once starved of their source, they will disappear by themselves.

See, we know that there is a law of cause and effect, which basically says that everything is caused by something else. If we get a cold, for example, it is because we contracted a virus. The cold does not just appears from nowhere, for no reason. We might not know the reasons, but they are always there. So it is wise, to look for the reason why something happens, rather than working hard to eliminate the effect, neglecting the cause.

See, most of the people believe that once they finish their school years, they need to learn no more, but the reality is that they learn daily. But not aware of this, they are not selective with the information that they come in contact with, to choose only what is beneficial for them. Every one of us is a specialist in something, depending on the work we do.

So, how come that we became specialists? We learned. And what is the result of our learning? We make enough money to survive, right? How about learning a little bit more, and become specialists in knowing ourselves, so we might be able to get rid of the stress that is producing so much misery in our life.

And we do not need to go to college for many years, or spend a fortune to do that.

Let me ask you a simple question, to illustrate this:

In order for you to be a good driver, and benefit from using your car, do you have to know everything about the car?

No, but you need to know the most important things, and respect them. And as result, your life will be more enjoyable by using the car in the right way. The same thing happens in our case. To use our mind the right way, we need to learn the basics, and then respect these laws of the mind. The results will be amazing, almost unbelievable.

See, everything becomes simple, if we learn how properly to use them.

Remember the first time when you drove the car? Yes, it was a little bit scary, but soon after you started to master it, the things changed. And now, what advice you might give to others, who want to learn how to drive?

Well, it's a piece of cake, you may say.

And the truth is that it's not difficult, but relatively easy.

And as we mentioned before, to do that we need accurate knowledge to use with our reasoning ability, so we can get the real results. And, by doing that, stress would be no more something that we have to live with, but just an option.

Remember: " If it is to be, it's up to me"

So, up till now, we learned that emotions could be controlled, and eliminated, if we do it the right way. And we should stop being slaves to uncontrolled emotions that might make our life miserable. Remember, there are two kinds of people today.

The ones, which do the thinking for themselves, and are called: "Leaders".

And the others, who need somebody to do the thinking for them, and are called: "Followers". Which one would you like to be? We know that our mind controls our body, and if that's so, then who should control our mind? Should we let the environment to control our mind, and as result our body? Or we should learn how consciously to control our mind, and by doing that we control to a large degree the environment? You might know the saying:

"It's not what happens to you, but what you do with what happens to you"

We all have a choice, to let the environment to control us, or we could learn how to control it for our benefit. And the only way to eliminate stress is by learning how to control our mind and by extension the environment.

From this information, we could see that emotions play an important role in our life, because they determine our state of mind, or more accurately they are our state of mind. And even though it might be news for us, there is a relatively easy way to deal with them. The most important thing that is required from us is to want to do something about it. It's our responsibility to do that. And unless we do it for ourselves it will remain undone. As you may know by now, in order for anybody to do something, they need to have a desire to do that. But the desire will never come unless somebody is aware of such a possibility. And till now you were thought, that you have to "manage" these negative emotions, as long as you live. Now, getting a better understanding of reality, it's up to you to take the necessary decisions to do something about it.

Through this information, we have seen that there is a way to eliminate stress, by stop forming new stress. And we do that by changing our understanding of it, how it is created, and our role in it. Realizing that is ourselves who are creating it, we are changing our behavior in such a way that the result of it is no more stress. In other words, we become stress free persons.

Now, let's see what can we do about the "stress that is already formed and is stored in our "memory " so to speak.

Chapter 7.

HOW TO REMOVE THE STRESS ALREADY FORMED.

Most of us have experienced many different situations that brought a lot of stress over us, not knowing where this stress is coming from. Seems like it comes from nowhere, hits us without mercy, and after we suffer for a while it goes away, but never forgets to come back later on. The psychologists call these cycles of stress depressions, or anxiety, because they seem to follow certain patterns, which repeat themselves from time to time.

The reality is, that these are the result of relieving the old stress that "was stored in our memory", and unconsciously is retrieved for some reason.

We have learned earlier, the way our mind works, is forming these neuron associations, which are stored in our memory, and used as reference in the decision making process. And during our life we have unconsciously made many negative associations that were stored in our memory, like files are stored in a computer. And every time when consciously or not, we retrieve any of these, we start to relive the same kind of feelings we have previously associated in the past. And when we are going through these cycles of stress, what we basically do, is we are retrieving files from our memory, and if they contain negative emotions or feelings attached to them, we automatically start to feel them, which of course have a stressful effect over us. And to make a situation worst, unaware of, we "save" these files, by storing them in our memory, so next time they could be retrieved again. And the whole cycle starts again and again.

But, if we have a computer, which for some reason contains many files that we might not like, what can we do about them? Well, you're right, we can delete, modify, or remove them. The good news is, that we also can do the same thing with any files from our memory.

It seems strange to you? We may not be able to change the audio or video information, from these neuron associations.

89

Because we cannot turn back the time, and go back in the past and relieve them in a different way. But, we can remove and replace the meaning we previously have given, to these past experiences. That is possible to do, and basically this is needed to remove the old stress. And, this is something that we do almost everyday, we are just not aware of it.

Let's take a simple example to illustrate this:

Suppose that you have to go on a business trip, to a different city. And of course, you have to stay there over night, so you get

to a hotel to rest till next day, when you have your appointment. You have your briefcase with many of your documents with you.

In the way from the airport you take a cab to the hotel, and once you get there, because you have to go to the rest room, you forget your briefcase in the back of the cab. After you get out of the rest room, suddenly you realize that the briefcase is missing, you go back outside the hotel, but the cab is gone, and of course all your documents needed for your meeting, are gone also.

Well, a stressful situation you might say. And like most of the people, you start to get worried. What is going to happen tomorrow at the meeting, without the needed documents? You try to find the cab driver by calling around, but no success. The cab driver vanished, and your briefcase too. Well, what kind of feelings do you start to associate about this situation? Most probably not positives, and staying at the hotel becomes an unpleasant experience. Next day you get ready for your appointment, get into the lobby to call for a cab, and then suddenly the unbelievable happens. The cab driver that brought you yesterday shows up, and with a smiling voice, hands you the briefcase, saying:

Sorry for this, Sir, but I just found your briefcase this morning, and I knew that you might be glad to have it back, so here I am with it.

What a relief this is for you. That whole tension and stress, suddenly disappears in a second. And gladly, you get into the cab, and so on.

What can we learn from this example? Well, by you giving a negative meaning to the situation, automatically it starts to affect you in a negative way. Now, if the cab driver never would have come back, then you might still have even today the same feelings, when you would remember about this situation. But, once you got positive information coming in - the cab driver bringing the briefcase- you changed instantly your mood, from a negative, to a positive one.

Did you need any medication, or to spend a large sum of money to do that? Of course not, you just reacted instantly. So, the possibility is there, you just have to act on it.

Now, let's say that the possibility is not there. What can you do? Well, you may consciously create one.

Remember, the subconscious mind cannot differentiate between real or fictional information. It will accept as truth, any information that we might choose to believe to be truth.

And, the point we are making here is that we have the capacity of removing and replacing a feeling with another one. If we can do it unconsciously, then we can learn to do it consciously also.

Now let's see how can we consciously remove and replace the negative emotions, and how to eliminate the stress, that we previously formed and "stored" in our memory. There are two ways to do that.

1. Removing one at a time, as we identify it.

2. Making a list with all the so called "stress ors", and removing them, one by one.

Let's take the first case:

1. REMOVING ONE AT A TIME, AS WE INDENTIFY IT.

In order for us to do that, we need to learn how to identify the potential stress ors, before they hit us, and we have no control over them. Remember, when a file is retrieved what we basically do, is we give a command to our mind to open the file, not to modify it. Knowing now that there are two possibilities to cause stress, (one by giving a negative meaning to the environment, and second by reliving old stress that was stored in our memory) we need to learn a habit of asking ourselves these questions:

Am I producing new stress, by giving a new negative meaning to this event or information? Or I am reliving a past negative memory?

Well, if we are not consciously giving a negative meaning to the information or event, then we are basically reliving a memory from the past that has a negative feeling attached to it. As we mentioned before, when the files are opened for reviewing, if we do not replace the negative meaning attached to them, they will be "stored back" in our memory, so next time they will have the same effect, or even more over us. Now, of course that, is till we master the habit of asking ourselves these two questions, we still experience stress that we might relieve, but as soon as we start to master it, it will be triggered automatically by our subconscious mind, right before we are to go into a stressful situation. And if we know in advance, before the negative feeling takes over, it's easy to reason the situation. You might know the saying:

"If the master of the house knows the time when the thief is striking, he will be vigilant, and stop him from robbing his house".

The same thing happens with us, when it comes to stress. Once the subconscious mind has this information in, it will, trigger

these questions in our mind before we start to get stressed so we might be able to consciously take the right steps to eliminate any negative outcome. As result, there will be no more new stress attached, or old stress saved for the future, to be retrieved, and felt later on. Basically, we do the same process with many other things. For example:

Do you remember when you have driven a car for the first time? Did you drive it with the same certainty as you do it now? Of course you did not. But, how long did you need to practice, till you started to master it? Most probably depended on how powerful your desire to drive was. Right?

What will you do now, if you drive the car in a school zone? Will you drive fast, or slow? Most probably, you will drive slowly. Why is that? Beside the fact that you are afraid of getting a ticket, you are aware of potential danger when kids are present. That's why your subconscious mind triggers the defense mechanism and makes you instantly slow down, as soon as you realize that you are driving in the school zone. Well, the same thing in our case. The higher the desire to eliminate stress, the faster we start to master it. And as in the case with the car, it is triggered before we enter a potential stressful situation, giving us the possibility to consciously choose what to do. Then, we could do the same old thing, and of course we get stress again, or remove the old negative meaning that used to result in our getting stressed.

Remember: "If it is to be, it's up to me" So, how do we remove the old stress? First we learn a habit of asking ourselves the question: Am I producing new stress now, or I am relieving an old one? If we find ourselves giving a negative meaning to the new information, we are producing new stress. But if we are not doing that, then we are experiencing an old stress retrieved from our memory. Once identified, we start to use positive reasoning, and as result, there will be no more stress to feel. And of course that same memory that previously had attached to it a negative meaning, will be replaced with a positive one. Next time when it will be retrieved, the feeling that will be felt will be positive.

2. MAKING A LIST WITH ALL THE SO-CALLED "STRESS ORS", AND TAKING ONE BY ONE.

Now let's go to the second method of removing the old stress

Well, this method is very simple, but requires a little bit of time and discipline. But since eliminating stress might be a priority for us, then there should not be any problem to do that.

So, what we need to do is, take a piece of paper, and make a list with all stress ors that we might remember: people, places events, anything that we know that have stressed us in the past. After we finished, we might rearrange them in three columns:

1. People that might be stress ors for us.

2. Places, or things that might be stress ors for us.

3. Events, or situations that might be stress ors for us.

Let's take one at the time, and start with people.

1. People that might be stress ors for us.

Suppose, that there are a few people in our life that any time we see or hear about them, we start to get nervous and stressed. And, because we have no choice, but have to interact with them physically or not, they present for us a reason to get stressed.

What can we do now? We might say. Remember Nathan's expression?

"They made my do it".

So, in our opinion, these people are the causes of our stress. But, also we remember what we have learned, why we actually get stressed. Not because of them, but because we are producing new stress, or we are reliving an old stress.

Now, is that particular person here? Let's say no. Then, the reason we start to feel that way, is because we are relieving the old stress, which was previously "stored" in our memory.

So, what we need to do is to replace these negative associations from this particular memory with a different feeling, which could be of love, pity, sorrow, or indifference. And, we do that by starting to use positive reasoning by asking few simple questions:

Are these persons aware, that they are causing me stress?

Do they willingly want to hurt me?

Even it might be so, should I let them control my feelings, or should I feel the way I want to feel?

Is my health and happiness more important than who is right or wrong?

Should I sacrifice my health, just to prove to somebody who does not appreciate me, that I am right and he is wrong?

Should I rather be happy, or right?

Should I still want these people to be a cause of stress for me, or should I forgive them?

By honestly answering these questions, what we basically do, is, we are removing these negative associations toward these peoples, and replacing them with different kind, that are not stress producing.

Let's take an example to illustrate this:

Suppose that you had a friend in high school, and you thought that he was a good friend of yours. After a while you were surprised to find out that he took something from you, without telling about it. And when you confronted him about this, he lied to you. Knowing that he did that, every time you see him, you might start to feel uncomfortable, and a negative feeling starts to develop in your mind. Well, you could keep doing the same old thing, and get the same old results, or you could use these questions, and remove these negative feelings from your memory.

See, the reality is that anytime when we associate a negative feeling towards somebody or something, we basically punish ourselves first, because these negative associations are stored in our mind, not theirs; and, we are the ones who get stressed when they are retrieved later on. By forgiving our "enemy" we basically do ourselves a big favor. We avoid forming a negative association that eventually will result in stress.

Let me ask you a question:

You might know that Jesus Christ taught his disciples to love their enemies? Do you think that he cared more for his disciples, or for the enemies?

The truth of the matter is, that knowing the damaging effect of these negative associations, he wanted his disciples to protect themselves from these harmful negative association that are formed in the mind, when somebody gives a negative meaning to the persons or events that they have to interact with. That's why He told them to love their enemy, in other words it does not matter who the enemy are, they should not have any control over the disciple's mind.

If the enemies do not know how to conduct themselves, and let the anger and cruelty govern their thinking, as His disciples, they should learn better.

So, we can learn to do the same, and the favor we do, is ours.

The "enemy" may still be enemy, we might not be able to change that, but we can change the way we feel about them, because our state of mind depends not on what they are, but on what we feel about them.

Let me tell you a little story that might illustrate this point:

A ten years old kid spends his summer vacation with his grandparents. And every morning, his grandpa takes him for a walk, and also to buy the morning newspaper, two blocks away from their house. And there was a salesman, at that particular store, who always was impolite with grandpa. After a while the kid asked him saying:

Grandpa, how come this person is so impolite with you, but you still are always nice to him? At this, grandpa, smiling, turned to the boy and answers: He is what he is, but this does not stops me from being a gentleman all the time. And why should I let him to control the way I feel? Maybe he does not know better, but I do. Let's take another example:

How do you feel, when you see one of your enemies?

Not good, right?

How do you feel, when you see a disabled person? Pity, right?

Which one would you like to help, a disabled person, or an enemy?

Well, of course, a disabled person.

Now, it might be hard for you to love your enemy, but can you show a kindness to a disabled person?

Yes.

Why do you think that the person you consider as enemy might act that way?

Most probably he does not know better, in other words is like a disabled person that because of his disability, cannot function normally.

Do you think that if your enemy might act like you, would he still be your enemy? Probably not.

And we can say that, not being like you, he is like somebody who is missing something to function properly, or act normally.

And that being the case, you could look at him as to a disabled person.

So, learn this habit of looking at your former enemy as you look to a disabled, or handicapped person. Once you do that, all the negative feeling will start to disappear.

Remember: Do you want to be a gentleman? Then no matter what the other might be, you stay a gentleman. If somebody wants to be a fool, why should you have to be one also? You don't have to. And by acting this way, you are protecting yourself, from the negative effects of the stress that are produced by these "stress ors."

From this information we can easily see that, we should be the ones to control the way we feel, and not others. I think we are smart enough to know, that we care more about ourselves, than others might do. Should we let the quality of our feelings to be determinate by them, or by us?

After we have finished with the list, we take again one at the time and review them, trusting ourselves that we are able to accomplish these changes. Remember, the subconscious mind accepts as truth anything that we consciously want to believe as truth, and acts on that information. So, we believe that these negative associations were removed and replaced with different ones. Next time when the same information might be retrieved by our subconscious mind, we start to feel the new feelings that we have attached to them. The old ones are gone forever, unless we start to reverse the process, and start to use negative reasoning again.

Now let's go to the second column with stress ors.

2.   Places, or things that might be stress ors for us.

We have seen how to deal with people, now let's see what can we do about the second category of so-called "old stress ors".

First let's identify them, so we know what are we dealing with.

For many of us, because of certain factors out of our control, many things or places little by little start to become stress ors. Our job, the house payments, car payments, medical bills, and some other payments, became a source of stress when we remember about them.

And all of us might want a solution for these. Well, we must remember that we were taught that stress cannot be eliminated, and we have to live with it. So, unaware of it, instead of looking how to eliminate this stressful effect of these things, our tendency was to run away from them. But no more, like any other stress ors, since we had them put together, we also are able to take them apart. Let's see how these became stress ors.

Were they stress ors from the beginning? Of course not.

Remember how excited were you, in the beginning when you got the job?

Finally, you are going to have your own money, to be free to spend them, the way you want. You were anxious to go to work. Or, do you remember after you bought your first car, or house, how proud were you writing the check for the payment, knowing that you do it, for your own car, or house?

Surly you might remember.

So, your attitude about these payments, were positive in the beginning.

But, because things started to change, the economy started to go down, the bills to pile up, little by little, you started unconsciously to replace these original positive feelings with negative ones. And after years of difficult situations, the level of negative feelings that you have attached to these became so high, that any time you have to deal with them they became for you a source of stress.

Now, remember, not the bills or the job, are the ones that stresses you, but the negative feelings, that you have attached to them. So, now you learn how to remove them, and once removed, they have no more stressful effect over you. Remember how these negative associations came to be? You used negative reasoning. So, to remove them, you need to take one at the time, and use positive reasoning, looking for what's good about them, and start to appreciate that. Once you have done that, all these negative feelings will be removed, and new ones will be made, which have no negative effect over you. Consciously believing that, the subconscious minds accept them as truth and acts accordingly.

As in the case with people, after you finished the whole list, you take again one at the time, review them and strengthen your new feelings attached to them. Next time when you have to deal with them, that negative feeling is gone, no more. Remember what they say in the medical field:

"The proper diagnostic is half the cure"

The same thing here, once properly identified, removing them is easy.

Let's go now, to see how to deal with the third column of old stress from our memory.

3.   Events, or situations that might be stress ors for us.

Knowing how to deal with old stress produced as the result of your interaction with people and places, it becomes easier for you to deal with situations or events. For the simple reason that most of these situations, are created by people in different places. So what you need to do is, to divide the situations or events in two or three parts, separating the people and places. Then take one at the time, and use the previous methods we already learned to eliminate that old stress. After you finished them all, rephrase the whole situation, and repeat it to yourselves. By doing this, next time when you go through the same situations, the old feeling of stress will be gone. You will experience the new feeling that you have attached to them.

Remember, when you work with a file in the computer, and you modify and save the work, what's going to happen when you review that particular file later on? Will you see, the old file? Or the new one? For sure that the old was replaced by the new one. The computer was designed to obey the last command. The same thing happens with our mind. Once we willingly remove the negative feelings and replace them with different ones, by saving them in our memory, next time when they are retrieved, will be the new one, the old ones are gone forever, unless we want to undo, what we have previously done.

Let's take an example to illustrate this:

Suppose that our job is a very stressful environment, because of the coworkers, and the volume of work that we have to accomplish in short periods of time. The situation makes us nervous and we start many times to argue with the boss. Then when we come home, not getting enough money, the situation becomes even more difficult, not being able to provide all the necessary things for the family. And so on. So, what can we do about it? We have learned previously, that beside the new stress that we might form on the spot, by giving a negative meaning to the environment, also we have an old stress stored in our memory that is retrieved for some reason or another. So, we divide the situation in two, people that stresses us and places, which in our case are, coworkers and family members, then our home and the working place.

Taking one at the time, we go through the same kind of questions that we have previously learned, and give an appropriate answer to them.

Should I let these people to control the way I feel? Or I am responsible for my own feelings?

Do they really want to stress me?

If this is what they know, should I know better?

100

Is there anything good about these situations I might benefit from?

Should I keep looking for the bad out of this situation and harm myself? Or I should appreciate myself enough to use a positive reasoning, with positive results, rather than act the old wrong way, and hurt myself or others?

An honest answer to these questions will help us to realize that it does not matter how difficult a situation might appear to be, there is still a positive side to it. And instead of looking for the negative, we learn this habit of looking for positive, and of course that the outcome will be totally different. So, what we basically do is to use positive reasoning, and as result we get positive feelings, which are going to replace the negative ones that were previously attached to these situations. Remember, your feelings are determined by the way you look at situations or events, not by the way they might really be. There are always two sides to any story, why not choose the good side of it, instead of the bad one? Are you afraid of getting too happy? I don't think so, and neither do you.

By now you realize that it is just foolish to keep using negative reasoning, knowing that as a outcome, this kind of reasoning will bring you only negative emotions, whatever they might be.

To do that, is like somebody has a choice of accepting in his house any person he might want. And for some reasons, he keeps inviting enemies, and then starts to complain how miserable his life becomes because of them. And next time, he does the same. Brings in again the enemy, and of course that the complaints keep coming. Well, now you know better, shouldn't you behave better?

By inviting different kind of people, friends who will make your life more enjoyable?

Or, because most of the people keep doing the old wrong thing, you have to do the same?

Remember:
"If you keep doing what were you doing, you'll keep getting what you were getting".

101

Chapter 8.

4.   MAKE UP YOUR MIND.

Now, after we realized that we as humans, are more than people that are struggling to survive, coming from nowhere, and going to the same place, now is the time to take a stand and seriously looking to our own existence, and take the responsibility of choosing the way we want to live our life. If in the past we lived, like most others do, just surviving, without being able to control our destiny, now is the time to wake up and realize, that if we do not do it for ourselves, nobody else will do it for us. Most of the people today, live in darkness, in regards to their destiny and purpose in life.

We all know, that we are superior to any other creature on earth today, but what we do with our superior abilities?   We damage our health, and destroy each other.

Did you ever see any of these other forms of life getting stressed, and inflicting so much pain and suffering to each other, as we do to ourselves, and others?

Look at the sky in a cloudless night.

Do you see the peace and harmony that exists over there?

Take a vacation, and go to the mountains.

Do you see how all of nature's components complement each other?

Do you see that all the animals, plants and other creatures know and respect their place in the cycle of nature?

Everything works as a unit, even though none of them have these abilities that we are equipped with.   And we, who are more superior than they, many times make our life and other's an unpleasant or even miserable journey.

Why is that?

Why, being so capable, are we still not able to create a happy society, so all together with nature we can enjoy a wonderful life as one specie, the human specie?

103

Well, the main reason is, that even though we might posses these wonderful abilities, we fail to look for the way they were designed to be used. And many times, in our desire to control everything around us, we forget that, we should learn to control ourselves first, and then to control the environment or others. We just forget to recognize a fundamental truth:

"There is no intelligent design, without an intelligent designer."

And instead of looking to understand what was the designer's purpose with us, and this unit we call earth, we follow our own ideas. And even though these abilities that we posses are very good, they do much damage, and produce pain and sorrow to many of us.

So, it might be useful to recognize, that we need to look for the purpose of our existence here on earth, and how properly we should use these abilities we were equipped with. There is more to life, than eating and drinking. It's up to us to look for the real answer. And for those who realize the importance of looking for the truth, they will find the real answers.

If the other forms of life, even though are not aware of their existence, are able to harmoniously participate to the perfect functionality of our earth, we should also conclude, that we who are more superior than they, should enjoy, and harmoniously participate, by doing our share, to maintaining the order and harmony on earth today.

Did you ever have the chance to see an aerial picture of our earth from space?

If you did, most probably you saw a peaceful and wonderful planet. The only one in the universe that is totally different than the rest. All the others are empty, and lifeless, only our earth is alive. Are we doing our best to maintain this peace and harmony as it could be seen from space?

Or, as many others do, we just do not care. Well, it's our individual duty to learn how to use these abilities we have, so together with all the other life forms here on earth, we maintain and build a future for ourselves, and our children.

Understanding the reasons and the functionality of our earth as a whole will help us to harmoniously work together with all other components to the peace and happiness of our entire existence. You have nothing to lose by learning about yourself and your abilities, but only to gain, for you, and the ones you love.

Remember, if the powerful designer had the power, wisdom, justice, and love to set up the whole universe, according to the laws and principles that we all see, he has for sure a plan with this earth and also with us. It's up to us to look to find out his purpose, and arrange our life to fit that purpose, instead of neglecting the most important part of our life: our future.